T0327893

APPALACHIAN
FOLKLORE UNVEILED

APPALACHIAN
FOLKLORE UNVEILED

MYSTERIOUS HAPPENINGS OF FOLK SPIRITS AND MYSTIC SHADES FROM THE ANCIENT FOOTHILLS

DARKNESS PREVAILS
WITH CARMAN CARRION

castle

CONTENTS

INTRODUCTION

Nestled within the heart of America lies a realm where the boundaries between reality and legend blur. A land of ancient mountains, whispering forests, and timeless traditions, the Appalachian region has given birth to a tapestry of folklore as rich and diverse as the very soil beneath its rugged terrain.

As a host of the *Freaky Folklore* podcast, I have had the privilege of delving into these hidden stories, venturing into the shadows, and peeling back the layers of mystery that shroud this enigmatic land. With the invaluable assistance of the esteemed owner of the Eeriecast Network, Darkness Prevails, our journey through the realms of Appalachian ghost stories has revealed a gilded treasury of folklore, culture,

and unexplained phenomena. It is my pleasure to share this with you—to bring you the little-known secrets, the dark and mysterious spaces, and the realm of the unknown.

Appalachia, a land steeped in tradition and resilience, has long been a crucible for stories of the unexplained. Its lush forests, rolling mountains, and secluded valleys have borne witness to generations of chilling encounters, each tale passed down through whispered words and shared around flickering campfires. In these pages, we will continue the storytelling tradition and embark on a chilling odyssey into the heart of the Appalachian wilderness. Here, you will encounter restless spirits that roam forgotten cemeteries, legendary cryptids that haunt the dense undergrowth, and otherworldly creatures that defy explanation. As we delve into these tales of terror, you will discover the cultural nuances and historical influences that have shaped these stories over the centuries.

This is more than just a collection of ghostly encounters; it is a journey into the very soul of a region that has borne witness to both beauty and darkness. With each story, you will gain insight into the beliefs, traditions, and superstitions that have been passed down through generations, painting a vivid picture of the people who came from around the world to call these mountains home.

While it would take both a much larger book and the direct oral tradition of the people of Appalachia to fully encapsulate this

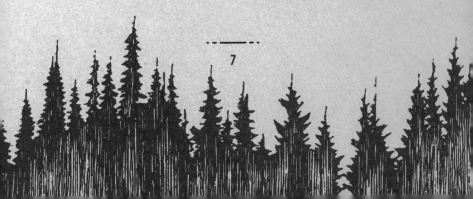

deep and diverse culture, here I also aim to shed light on an oft-misunderstood people. It is not lost on history that groups of people perceived as isolated often have assumptions and stereotypes made about them. This tendency may stem from a fear of the unknown, but it also highlights our innate mistake of oversimplifying cultures by failing to apply proper context. Despite common misconceptions, regions like Appalachia, while mountainous, were never truly cut off from trade or outside influences. Appalachia has been subjected to many unflattering stereotypes over time, perpetuated by pop culture through movies like *Deliverance* (Warner Bros., 1972) in which the people of this region have been warped into being violent and fearsome, and at best, unpredictable and unreasonable. While many, if not most, remote cultures have suffered similar misrepresentations, it is my hope to shed light on these dark assumptions and unveil a beautifully rich culture deeply steeped in time, landscape, and diverse perspectives. It is my goal to show you a people wrapped in legend, tied to family, supportive of the community, self-reliant and strong, innovative and traditional, passionate and creative, and morally sound.

Prepare to be enchanted, enthralled, and terrified in equal measure as we journey into the heart of Appalachia, where the line between the living and the dead is as thin as the mist that clings to these haunted hills, lore comes to life, and the spirits refuse to rest. Now, I invite you to join me on a journey into the depths of Appalachian mystique as we explore its ghosts, legends, monsters, and more.

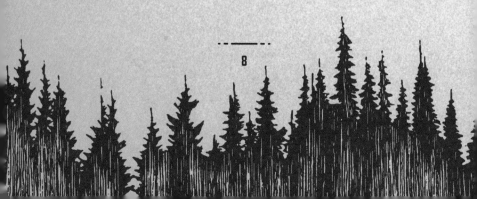

HISTORY, CULTURE, LEGENDS, AND INFLUENCES

The Appalachian Mountains, a formidable range that stretches from the Canadian region of Newfoundland and Labrador to the southern states of Alabama and Georgia, represent one of Earth's most ancient and enduring geological formations. Their emergence traces back approximately 480 million years, rendering them over five times older than their towering counterparts, the Rocky Mountains. The insistent passage of time and relentless forces of erosion have gradually whittled down these once-majestic peaks, believed by some to have rivaled the Himalayas and Mount Everest in their prime. Today, the region we collectively know as "Appalachia" is often categorized into three distinct regions: the Northern, Central, and Southern Appalachians. While the exact demarcation lines may be the subject of debate, what unifies these regions is the fabric of a shared history, culture, and folklore, each marked by its own distinct nuances.

HISTORY

It is worth dispelling a prevalent stereotype that often associates Appalachian culture primarily with poverty and a homogenously white population. In reality, the early pioneers who ventured into these mountains were a diverse group, comprised of Native Americans, newly arrived European settlers, and enslaved Africans. Native Americans were the original inhabitants of the Appalachian region, having lived there for thousands of years and developed rich, complex societies. European settlers began arriving in the 18th century, drawn by the promise of land and new opportunities; they included Scots-Irish, Germans, and English among others, each bringing their own customs and traditions. Africans arrived through the Transatlantic Slave Trade, forcibly brought to America and contributing significantly to the cultural and economic development of the region despite the harsh conditions they faced.

Before the arrival of European settlers, the Native American tribes in the Appalachian region possessed their own distinct cultural practices and oral traditions. In Southern Appalachia, the Cherokee Nation stood as the prominent Indigenous community and laid the very groundwork for the folklore of today. The Cherokee interpreted both the visible and veiled aspects of their world through a robust history of song and storytelling. The mysterious mist that frequently blanketed the

Great Smoky Mountains held a particular significance in their narratives, with echoes of these tales found in famous Appalachian ghost stories.

With the influx of European settlers, the Indigenous way of life underwent profound transformations. Early explorers, including the Spanish and French, began encroaching upon these lands as early as the 1500s. They were soon followed by waves of immigrants from the British Isles, particularly those of Scot-Irish descent. These settlers were known for their clannish nature and fierce independence, having rebelled against restrictive laws in their countries of origin. For them, the Appalachian region's dense hardwood forests full of game and pristine rivers brimming with fish offered both familiarity and opportunity, but also autonomy, which was highly sought after enduring centuries of land wars in Europe.

The integration of these cultures played a pivotal role in nurturing a sense of community among these early settlers. Activities like communal corn shucking, house raising, and log rolling served as gatherings that fostered bonds among neighbors, but it was the mountain dances and music that truly stood out as the epicenter of social interaction. In areas where local churches frowned upon dancing, these gatherings were often referred to as "play parties." Fiddlers, accompanied by banjo and dulcimer players, regaled the crowd with a repertoire that swung from humorous to melancholic, evoking memories of distant homelands. Often these musicians wove stories into their songs, recounting local legends, fairy tales, and ghost stories. The popular Appalachian ghost story, "The Ghost of Fiddler's Rock," finds its origin in one of these musical soirées and demonstrates the importance of music to the people. It can be said that the story also stands as a cautionary tale about being greedy and abusing natural resources.

As the story goes, around the turn of the century, a young man in the hills of East Tennessee named Martin Stone would roam the rough and deserted back roads playing Old English ballads on his fiddle. He was well-known by the people of the mountain, and it was popular to hire him to play weddings, house raisings, holiday celebrations, and play parties. It was rumored that he played so sweetly that he could soothe crying babies and heal the sick, even waking before daylight to usher in the rising sun with song. Often, he would sit on the bluff, admiring his handiwork in the bright morning, playing his fiddle as the day grew long. One morning, as he played, snakes began to gather at his feet to sway to his music and bask in the warmth of the sun. Realizing that snake skins could make a pretty penny on the market, he crushed the largest snake under his boot, making more than a day's wage with that one killing (in some retellings, he comes back with a shotgun and kills many of the snakes at once).

As this was an easier way to make a living than play parties and weddings, he began coming to the bluff daily, using his music to lure the creatures to his feet for easy hunting. Making a killing during the day (so to speak) had Martin wondering if he could double his profits by also hunting the snakes at night. He headed up to the bluff when night fell, fiddle tuned and ready beneath his arm. The next morning, a local man noticed Martin's mule tied up near the ledge and thought it strange, as Martin was not typically known to stay overnight on the cliffs. He organized a search party, who eventually discovered Martin's body on the bluff, covered in snake bites, his face and arms swollen and blue with venom. To this day, the residents of Johnson County avoid Fiddler's Bluff, and some still hear the mournful wails of Martin's fiddle, once an instrument that gave voice to community joy now a distant and lonely cry.

CULTURE

Appalachia is known for its rugged, mountainous terrain, which historically posed challenges for rapid trade and communication with metropolitan areas where capitalism was rapidly evolving. Despite these geographic challenges, Appalachians were significantly involved in broader economic activities; by the early 20th century, 85 percent of all botanical drugs were sourced from the mountains. While the isolation affected the speed of trade, it did not make the residents more reliant on homesteading than other communities of the time.

This environment did encourage a degree of self-reliance: residents often grew their own food, built their own homes, and utilized local resources for survival. Many Appalachian families have a long tradition of living off the land by hunting, fishing, farming, and foraging, with these practices being passed down through generations. This fostered a strong sense of independence and tight-knit family bonds. Historically, the region faced economic challenges, including limited job opportunities, especially as the mining industry began to decline. This led many residents to become self-employed, running small farms or businesses that serviced local communities. The value placed on hard work, frugality, and the ability to handle adversity without relying on external support has been continuously reinforced through stories, songs, and oral traditions. This resourcefulness has become a defining characteristic of Appalachian culture.

The resourcefulness of Appalachians is evident in their ability to make the most of available resources and find creative solutions to challenges. This ingenuity extends to various aspects of life, including crafts, home remedies, homebuilding, and food preservation. Many Appalachians have historically adopted sustainable practices, such as growing heirloom crops, preserving traditional farming techniques, and using environmentally friendly methods. These practices often align with a practical approach to living off the land. Community support has always been a crucial aspect of Appalachian life. Neighbors frequently come together to help one another, fostering a strong sense of communal solidarity. This collective support complements individual efforts toward self-sufficiency and independence. Appalachians often take pride in their ability to solve problems and meet their needs without relying heavily on external assistance. Community stores, bartering, and sharing successful farming and sustainability techniques are common practices that enhance the resilience and cohesion of Appalachian communities. The region values its rich history, spirituality, and family connections, which contribute to a vibrant and thriving community life.

Historically, the region has experienced cycles of exploitation and neglect by outside forces, leading to skepticism of government intervention or aid. The people of Appalachia have shown remarkable adaptability in the face of change and adversity. This malleability and autonomy reflect an enduring, indestructible spirit in the face of all that life can bring and is evidenced by their indelible mark on American music, expert craftsmanship, skillful art, soulful poetry, multifarious cuisine, and enchanted folklore.

music

Appalachian music, a cornerstone of the culture, has left an everlasting mark on the broader landscape of American music. Musicians in the region—often equipped with banjos, fiddles, and mountain dulcimers—played a pivotal role in shaping bluegrass, country, and Americana folk music. Iconic figures like Bill Monroe, the Carter Family, and Doc Watson hail from Appalachia, their contributions resonating worldwide.

The ballads and folk songs of the region are not just musical compositions, but also a means of storytelling. These songs recount tales of love and heartbreak, the struggles of daily life, and the history of the region. They provide a moral compass and are a testament to the enduring spirit of the Appalachian people, who use music as a medium of expression and connection across generations.

The banjo can be considered the beating heart of Appalachian music and is, at the very least, a widely recognized aspect of Americana. It originated from West African gourds that had been turned into string instruments, and the concept was brought to the Americas by enslaved Africans during the Transatlantic Slave Trade (1501 to 1867). In developing Appalachian culture, the banjo played a significant role in shaping the region's distinct musical heritage. It became a key instrument, contributing to the development of bluegrass, old-time, and mountain music. The banjo's unique sound and versatility made it well-suited for the spirited, foot-stomping tunes that define the sound distinctive to the region. It is said that the ghosts of the forests enjoy music and will travel from afar to gather in groups to listen to mountain bands play.

While the mark that Appalachian music has made not only on the region but on the country as a whole is palpable, countless traditions contribute to shaping the identity of a people through art and craftsmanship.

QUILTING

Appalachian quilting stands as a vibrant and cherished tradition, weaving together stories, culture, and practicality in a tapestry of cloth. Rooted in the rugged hills and valleys of the Appalachian Mountains, this art form has not only provided warmth but has also stitched together the stories of generations.

Appalachian quilts, known for their intricate patterns and vibrant colors, are crafted by women of the region using scraps of fabric. These quilts serve as functional blankets and works of art, embodying the spirit of resourcefulness. The roots of Appalachian quilting stretch across centuries, intertwining the influences of European settlers, African American craftsmanship, and the practical needs of rural life. Quilting was an essential skill passed down through families, with each stitch telling a story of resilience and resourcefulness. Appalachian quilts boast a rich array of patterns, each carrying their own symbolism and history that are intimately tied to the families who create and utilize them. The Log Cabin pattern, for example, symbolizes the importance of home and hearth, while the Double Wedding Ring design reflects the interconnectedness of family bonds. Quilts with this pattern are often gifted to the newly betrothed. A star-patterned quilt on the bed will ward off evil spirits and nightmares. These patterns were often passed down through oral tradition, with families sharing their techniques and designs.

In the Appalachian tradition, quilting was not just an artistic expression but a pragmatic necessity. Quilts were crafted from scraps of fabric made from worn-out clothing, drapery, and remnants of other sewing projects. This resourcefulness added a layer of sustainability to the art, transforming utilitarian objects into intricate and colorful works of beauty. As such, quilting bees are a common social event in Appalachian communities.

At a quilting bee, women gather to quilt while sharing stories, laughter, and a sense of camaraderie. These gatherings not only strengthen social bonds but also provide a platform for the exchange of techniques and designs. Appalachian quilts often tell a story, documenting family history and featuring patches of fabric from important life events like weddings, births, or even deaths and losses—with each piece of fabric contributing to a larger narrative.

WOODWORKING

In the Appalachian Mountains, the art of woodworking is not just a necessary skill, it's a legacy. Renowned for their craftsmanship, Appalachian woodworkers have shaped a distinctive tradition that encompasses everything from functional furniture to soul-stirring musical instruments. The intricate carvings reflect the region's dedication to preserving traditional techniques.

The roots of Appalachian woodworking can be traced back to the early European settlers who brought their carpentry traditions to the rugged landscapes of Appalachia. These settlers relied on their skills to create essential items for daily life. As a result, the craft became deeply intertwined with the region's history and survival. From sturdy, handcrafted furniture that graces homes to useful items like chests, buckets, stools, ladders, cabinets, tools, and kitchen utensils, the craftsmanship is both practical and aesthetically pleasing. Each piece tells a story of necessity, creativity, and an intimate connection to natural resources.

One of the most enchanting aspects of Appalachian woodworking is its contribution to the world of music. Luthiers, skilled artisans specializing in stringed instrument construction, have long thrived in the region. Banjos, guitars, fiddles, and dulcimers crafted with precision and care resonate not only with melodious tunes but also with the spirit of the mountains preserved in the very wood used to create first the instrument, then the music. Carpentry techniques are often passed down within families or apprenticed by a master. Hand tools, such as chisels, planes, and drawknives, are revered for their role in shaping intricate details. The use of traditional joinery methods, such as dovetails and mortise and tenon, adds a level of durability and careful attention to detail to each creation while negating the reliance on factory-created tools. Regional woodworkers are known for their exquisite carvings and fine details that adorn furniture and instruments. The carvings often draw inspiration from nature, featuring motifs like leaves, vines, and wildlife. This connection to the natural surroundings is evident in every delicate detail, turning functional pieces into true works of art.

While preserving traditional techniques, Appalachian woodworkers also embrace contemporary innovations. Some artisans blend traditional designs with modern aesthetics, creating a harmonious balance between heritage and innovation. This adaptability ensures that the art of Appalachian woodworking remains relevant and continues to evolve by allowing room for invention. Carpentry in Appalachia is not a solitary pursuit; like quilting, it's often a communal activity. Woodworkers come together to share knowledge, swap ideas, and collaborate on projects. This sense of community fosters a supportive environment where skills are honed and traditions are upheld.

BASKET WEAVING

Basket weaving is another treasured craft in Appalachia, with artisans creating both practical and decorative baskets. These baskets serve as functional items and works of art that carry on the tradition of skilled craftsmanship. The art of basketry is a cherished tradition that weaves together history, utility, and artistic expression. The roots of Appalachian basket weaving stretch back to Native Americans, the early European settlers, and Africans, who tied their weaving traditions closely to the rugged landscapes that surrounded them by using readily available resources like reeds, grasses, vines, and twigs. Woven baskets serve essential roles in daily life, providing practical solutions for harvesting, storage, and transportation in the absence of factory-made containers.

Appalachian baskets are celebrated for their functional elegance. Crafted from locally sourced materials, such as native hardwoods, these baskets were designed with specific purposes in mind, which explains their varied shapes. Whether used for gathering crops, carrying goods to market, or storing household items, each basket bears the imprint of the artisan's skill and the community's needs. Appalachian basket weavers are known for producing a diverse array of basket forms, each adapted to a specific function. From large, sturdy egg baskets with wide handles to delicate, intricately woven fruit baskets, the variety showcases both the versatility of the craft and the resourcefulness of the artisans.

Beyond their practical uses, Appalachian baskets hold cultural and symbolic significance within the communities. They are crafted for specific occasions, such as weddings and births, or as gifts symbolizing friendship and goodwill. The act of weaving itself often becomes a communal activity, reinforcing social bonds and preserving a sense of shared heritage and history.

POTTERY

The art of pottery making in the Appalachian region is deeply rooted in the convergence of the various cultural influences that we've been discussing. Before European settlement, Indigenous American communities had a long lineage of pottery making through crafting functional items like cooking vessels, storage containers, and ceremonial pieces. The Cherokee, Creek, and other tribes in the area used local clays to create distinctive pottery characterized by unique shapes, intricate designs, and often vibrant colors.

With the arrival of European settlers, particularly those of German, English, and Scot-Irish descent, new pottery traditions were introduced to the region. European settlers brought their own techniques, glazing methods, and preferences for certain types of vessels.

Africans who were forced into America through slavery came to the region seeking to carve out a free and independent life, playing a distinct role in shaping the recognizable beauty of Appalachian pottery. They brought knowledge of traditional African pottery techniques and contributed to the diversity of styles in the region. The use of specific decorative elements and the incorporation of natural materials were highly influenced by African pottery traditions.

Appalachian pottery is known for its utilitarian purpose and simple, yet elegant, designs. Common forms include jars, jugs, crocks, and churns used for food storage and preservation. Many potters in the region developed signature glazes, such as alkaline and ash, which were often specific to certain geographic areas. This led to several communities becoming renowned for their pottery. The Seagrove area in North Carolina, for example, is known as the "Pottery Capital of the United States." Other notable pottery communities include Catawba Valley in North Carolina and Edgefield District in South Carolina.

CUISINE

Appalachian cuisine is a reflection of the region's varied cultures, history, available resources, self-sufficiency, and smashing good taste. It is hearty, flavorful, comforting, and a testament to making the most of what is at hand. Indigenous Americans, including Shawnee, Cherokee, and Choctaw, cultivated and foraged for a variety of foods, including corn, beans, squash, ramps, berries, wild game, and fish. Many of these ingredients became staples in local cuisine. Africans and their descendants in the region made significant contributions to the food culture when they brought their knowledge of cultivating crops like okra, black-eyed peas, and various leafy greens. The African influence is particularly notable in the "soul food" dishes that are a signature of Appalachian cooking. European immigrants—such as the Scots-Irish, English, German, and others—introduced cornmeal, which became a fundamental ingredient, and other pantry staples like apples, cabbage, and potatoes. Some iconic Appalachian dishes and foodways include:

Corn Bread and Buttermilk Biscuits

Corn bread and buttermilk biscuits are staples of Appalachian cuisine, often served with butter, honey, or gravy. These simple yet satisfying breads have been a mainstay of family tables for centuries.

Beans

Common, simple, and hearty, a meal of corn bread and beans has seemingly always been on Appalachian tables. Corn bread is often served with pinto beans, creating a nutritious and satisfying meal. Beans are appreciated for their storability and nutritional protein during the sparser winter months when hunting and fishing are less available to provide sustenance.

Apple Butter and Preserves

Making apple butter and preserves is a time-honored Appalachian practice. Apples are cooked slowly to create a sweet and spiced spread that can be enjoyed on bread or biscuits. Appalachian families have a long history of preserving food through canning and drying, due to their need to continue their self-sufficiency throughout the winter. This practice ensures that the bounty of the growing season can always be enjoyed.

Game Hunting

Wild game has always been integral to Appalachian cuisine, across all contributing cultures. Venison, rabbit, squirrel, and other wild meats are used in stews, pies, and countless savory dishes.

Fried Catfish and Trout

Given the abundance of rivers and lakes, fried catfish and trout are popular mainstays. The fish are often coated in cornmeal and fried to perfection in deep cast-iron skillets filled with fat from the hunted game.

Moonshine

Appalachians have a notable history of distilling high-proof
spirits, including whiskey, which is known as "moonshine."
While illegal for much of its history, the tradition of homemade
spirits has contributed to the unique culture of the region,
helped support families, especially in the slimmer months, and
reinforced their autonomy.

Sorghum

Molasses extracted from the sorghum cane is often used as a
sugar alternative, so sorghum molasses is a common household
staple. It is often drizzled over biscuits or used in baking. It is
also commonly used in granny magic and healing traditions.

Stack Cake

A traditional dessert, stack cake consists of layers of thin, molasses-rich cakes stacked together with apple butter or fruit preserves between each layer.

Hoecakes

Also known as johnny cakes or corn fritters, hoecakes are a simple type of corn bread cooked on a hoe (another word for a griddle), which have been a quick and easy staple in Appalachian kitchens for an anytime meal.

Fried Green Tomatoes

A classic southern Appalachian dish, fried young, green tomatoes often served as a side or a snack. The tartness of unripe tomatoes pairs well with a crispy cornmeal coating, and these can be served long before the ripening season.

Wild Edibles

Appalachia's abundant natural resources offer a wealth of seasonal wild edibles ripe for foraging, including ramps, morel and other types of mushrooms, wild onions and herbs, and a variety of berries, including blackberries. These ingredients often find their way into traditional dishes, both sweet and savory, intimately connecting the cuisine to the land.

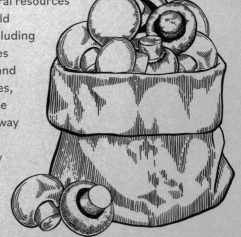

APPALACHIAN BUTTERMILK BISCUITS

I am of the belief that to truly know a culture, you must try the food. Here, I have included my favorite biscuit recipe. Of course, this can be made and eaten any time you please, but I encourage you to saddle up to a nice warm bowl of chili to dunk it in, or simply eat with butter, honey, or apple butter, as is tradition.

Ingredients:

2 cups (250 g) all-purpose flour

1 tablespoon baking powder

½ teaspoon baking soda

1 teaspoon salt

½ cup (1 stick, 115 g) cold unsalted butter, diced into small pieces, plus 1 to 2 tablespoons melted unsalted butter for brushing

1 cup (240 ml) buttermilk (or substitute with whole milk mixed with 1 tablespoon of vinegar or lemon juice)

Instructions:

1 Preheat your oven to 450°F (230°C)

2 In a mixing bowl, combine the all-purpose flour, baking powder, baking soda, and salt. Stir them together until well mixed.

3   Add the cold, diced butter to the dry ingredients. Use a pastry cutter or your fingers to work the butter into the flour mixture until it resembles coarse crumbs. The small butter pieces will create a flaky texture in the biscuits.

4   Pour in the buttermilk (or milk and vinegar mixture). Stir gently until the dough comes together. Be careful not to overmix; just combine the ingredients until a sticky dough forms.

5   Turn the dough out onto a floured surface. Knead it gently a few times, folding it over onto itself, and then pat it into a ½- to ¾-inch thick rectangle.

6   Place the biscuits on a baking sheet lined with parchment paper, making sure they are touching slightly for soft sides or spaced ½ inch apart for crispier sides.

7   Brush the tops of biscuits with melted butter. This will help them brown nicely in the oven.

8   Bake in the preheated oven for about 10-12 minutes, or until the biscuits are golden brown and have risen.

9   Once baked, remove them from the oven and serve warm with butter, honey, or your favorite jam.

LITERARY CONTRIBUTIONS

Reflecting a strong storytelling culture, one of the most profound ways that Appalachia makes its way into American culture as a whole is through its writers. Authors like Ron Rash and Charles Frazier explore the region's beauty and lore in their novels. These writers draw upon the region's landscapes, people, and stories to craft narratives that, although reflective of a society in isolation, resonate with readers worldwide, across time. Ron Rash, for instance, has been celebrated for his poignant and evocative storytelling, often set in the Appalachian Mountains. His novels, such as *Serena* (Ecco, 2009) and *One Foot in Eden* (Picador, 2003) delve into the complexities of human relationships, the impact of historical events, and the natural beauty of the region. Charles Frazier's acclaimed novel *Cold Mountain* (Vintage, 1998) is another example of a work that weaves the fabric of Appalachian life into a compelling and modern narrative.

It's interesting to examine how a culture so deeply rooted in time and place, relatively cut off from metropolitan life (whether by choice or by geography and climate), has such a rich living legacy that it pushes its way into contemporary urban lives. From music to food to visual arts to functional craftsmanship, it makes an indelible impact on many aspects of American culture as a whole. As long as the people of Appalachia cherish their traditions, values, and stories, this saga will endure, resonating with those who seek to understand the pioneering spirit of the region. It is a culture rooted in the land, nourished by community, and celebrated through the vibrant expressions of music, craft, and storytelling. Appalachia's unique heritage is proof of the resilience of its people and the enduring power of their culture.

INFLUENCES

The spiritual beliefs and mythologies of the Cherokee, Creek, Shawnee, and other Indigenous tribes deeply impacted regional folklore. Many Appalachian folktales and superstitions contain elements borrowed from Native American cosmologies. This influence can be seen in stories featuring powerful nature spirits and beings connected to the natural world that serve to explain the phenomena around them. Native Americans have an intimate and profound connection to the land. Their reverence for nature, coupled with their belief in the spiritual significance of natural elements—such as animals, trees, and bodies of water—left an indelible mark on local folklore. In many stories, nature is depicted as a living, breathing entity, filled with spirits and magic.

In general, Native American, African American, and European communities and cultures have a firm tradition of oral storytelling, which translates strongly in the people of the region and their way of life. The art of passing down stories through generations to preserve history and wisdom was shared across groups. They shared myths, legends, fairy tales, and folktales from their respective homelands, elements that blended over time. Belief in witchcraft, herbal remedies, and omens were common and often intertwined with Christian beliefs. These superstitions and tales, rooted in cultural tradition, continue to influence Appalachian practices and folklore.

CREATURES AND SPIRITS

There is an abundance of creatures and spirits in Appalachian folklore, which can be attributed to several factors, including the region's cultural diversity, historical influences, and the natural landscape of the mountains. The Cherokee people, among other Native American tribes, have contributed enduring elements such as nature spirits, animal spirits, and trickster figures to the mix. The concept of "little people" in Cherokee legends, much like European fairies, may have influenced stories of diminutive beings in folklore.

Freed and escaped enslaved Africans and their descendants contributed elements like conjure, rootwork, and stories of haints and spirits that were born in the land from which they were originally ripped. The concept of "boo hags," or witches who ride people's chests at night, for instance, likely has African roots. German and Dutch immigrants introduced elements of their own, such as the full moon shapeshifters known as werewolves. The concept of "holler witching"— using supernatural powers to harm others—is believed to have Germanic tribal origins. The unique topography and bioregional challenges of the Appalachian Mountains influenced the evolution of local folklore. These settings fostered the emergence and adaptation of new creatures and spirits, reflecting the specific environmental and cultural conditions of mountain life. Despite the movement of books, goods, and people in and out of the region, these influences contributed to a distinct and rich folkloric tradition.

Nature Spirits
Native American tribes held profound reverence for nature spirits inhabiting forests, rivers, and mountains. In Appalachian folklore, nature spirits and beings tied to the land feature

prominently. These entities, such as forest sprites or river nymphs, reflect the belief in the spiritual presence of the natural world, a concept strongly inherited from Native American cultures but influenced by European and Old English tales of fairies. Yunwi Tsunsdi, meaning "little people," are Cherokee nature spirits who present as child-sized humanoids and can be considered fairies. They are kind and often help people, but are very defensive of the natural world, so they can be dangerous to humans who disrespect them or the landscape.

Ancestral Spirits
Appalachian communities share a deep respect for ancestral spirits. It is common to believe that the spirits of deceased loved ones continue to watch over and protect the living. The concept of ancestral spirits in Appalachian ghost stories reflects the influence of Native American beliefs in the enduring connection between the living and the dead.

Guardian Spirits
Appalachian cultures often believe in guardian spirits associated with specific individuals or clans. These guardians were protective and offered guidance. In some ghost stories, the presence of guardian spirits or protective entities is evident, mirroring the Native American belief in spiritual protectors. The red-tailed hawk is said to be the guardian spirit of the Cherokee people.

Shapeshifters and Animal Spirits
Native American folklore often features shapeshifters and animal spirits that can take on human or animal forms. These concepts found their way into Appalachian lore in the form of creatures that could assume various shapes or have strong likenesses of and connections to animals. The Cherokee Raven Mocker is a great example of an Appalachian shapeshifter.

Hailing from southwest Virginia, this birdlike monster, with its black feathers and humanoid strong arms and legs, trolls the land looking for livestock, wildlife, or human hearts to eat. This monster can take the form of a bird in flight but is also often seen as an elderly man or woman. When in human form, the Raven Mocker can sneak up on unsuspecting people and eat their hearts right from their chests without them even noticing.

NATURE-BASED OMENS

Both Indigenous cultures and Appalachian communities as a whole believe that animals can act as messengers or omens. The symbolism of certain animals and their behaviors in Native American traditions influenced the interpretation of animal omens in Appalachia. For example, the call of certain birds or the sighting of specific animals might be seen as harbingers of good or bad fortune.

Observations of the natural world, such as weather patterns, cloud formations, or celestial events were believed to foreshadow outcomes or serve as omens. Signs that it's going to be a particularly difficult and cold winter might be if corn is hard to shuck, if corn silk is unusually thick, if a caterpillar spotted in the fall has yellow on its nose, or if the bark is extra thick on the north side of a tree.

SACRED SITES AND HAUNTINGS

Sacred sites and burial mounds are scattered throughout
the Appalachian region. These became intertwined with
local folklore, with tales of hauntings, guardian spirits, and
mystical occurrences associated with them. The belief in
spirits inhabiting these sacred places influenced ghost stories
centered around similar locations and the land. The hauntings
tend to be caused by local folk heroes, lost Civil War soldiers,
wandering souls, and spirits of the dead.

In the Appalachian Mountains of North Carolina, near the
town of Hot Springs, lies a scenic overlook known as Lover's
Leap. This site is steeped in local legend, telling the tale of a
young Cherokee couple whose love was forbidden by their
warring families. Desperate to be together, they chose to leap
from the cliff into the French Broad River below rather than
be separated. The spirits of the lovers are said to still linger,

and those who visit the site sometimes claim to see their spectral figures or hear their mournful whispers in the wind. The story of Lover's Leap has been passed down through generations, contributing to the rich tapestry of folklore in the Appalachian region and drawing visitors who seek to experience its poignant history and breathtaking views.

FOLKLORE AND LEGENDS

In Appalachian folklore, omens and signs hold great significance, playing a multifaceted role in the lives of the people. These signs and portents are deeply woven into the region's culture. They are often interpreted as guidance from the spiritual or natural world. They are seen as real-time messages that can help individuals make decisions, predict future events, navigate their lives, and signal significant happenings.

Appalachian folklore features a variety of legendary beings, often rooted in the land and nature. These beings, such as ghostly wandering Civil War soldiers and Mothman, reflect the influence of strong cultural heritage from many angles. They embody the belief in mystical creatures that inhabit the wild and untamed landscapes of the region, stories that are often truly believed in.

NATIVE AMERICAN LEGENDS

Native American cultures have a rich tradition of legends and myths that feature a wide array of mythical beings, gods, and heroes. These legends often drew upon the natural world and the spirits inhabiting it. A good example of this is the Moon-Eyed People, who were said to be short, fat, bearded, white-skinned men. They were called "moon-eyed" because they had poor eyesight in the daytime.

As told by European settler accounts, the Cherokee expelled these curious creatures from the region and brought peace back to the residents. The story often involves conflict with the Creek tribe, when a particular night with a bright full moon allowed the Creeks to ambush the Moon-Eyed People, taking advantage of their poor eyesight in bright light. This attack supposedly left the Moon-Eyed People defenseless, leading to their displacement. Additionally, other versions of the story tell of the Cherokee driving the Moon-Eyed People westward into what is now Tennessee.

AFRICAN LEGENDS

African folklore is rich with a diverse array of spirits, deities, and supernatural beings. Some of these figures, such as spirits of nature, ancestors, and trickster deities, have found their way into Appalachian legends. The melding of these supernatural entities with European and Native American beliefs has given rise to stories of unique mythical beings in the region. African influences on lore often involved themes of triumph over oppression and evil, independence, dishonesty, and ethics. Anansi is a story brought to the Southern United States by enslaved West Africans and tells the tale of a spider who was able to stay alive (despite his tiny size) by using his wits to outsmart those who might crush him, tricking his oppressors into their own demise.

EUROPEAN LEGENDS

The early European settlers' cultural beliefs, folklore, and traditions merged with the existing Native American and African influences in the region, contributing to the creation of a distinctive cultural folklore. They brought their homeland's stories of mythical creatures, heroes, and supernatural beings, such as fairies, elves, trolls, leprechauns, and gnomes. Fairies, or "fair folk" in Appalachia, are reminiscent of Old English and Celtic lore, where these creatures appear in ancient stories as tricksters and are often friends to humans. In Appalachia, they are masters of the land and are thanked after a successful hunt, honored for the mushrooms and berries that are ripe for foraging, and acknowledged as the givers of gifts of the land.

If you stumble upon a ring of mushrooms on the forest floor, this indicates a spot where the fair folk have been dancing in a circle. Stand in the center of the ring and make a wish and it'll be sure to come true.

WEAVING APPALACHIAN FOLKLORE

Folktales, omens, superstitions, and legends connect the people of the region to their ancestral past and steadfast belief in the supernatural, serving as a bridge between distinct but intertwined cultures. Indeed, the cultural diversity of Appalachia weaves a captivating tapestry of folklore; it is a testament to the varied traditions, beliefs, histories, and experiences that have shaped the region's culture over centuries.

The story of the Nûñnë'hï is an example of a shared legend that demonstrates the cultural diversity and interplay of various influences in Appalachian folklore. In Cherokee lore, the Nûñnë'hï are typically described as small-statured, otherworldly people who are often hidden from human sight. They are believed to have the ability to appear and disappear at will, making them very difficult to encounter. Despite their small stature, the Nûñnë'hï are known for their incredible strength and fierce protectiveness of the landscape. The Nûñnë'hï are closely associated with the natural world, and they are considered to be the "People Who Live Anywhere" or the "Invisible People." It is believed that they reside within the mountains, forests, and caves of the Appalachians Mountains. They are said to have a strong affinity for wildlife and the environment, and serve as guardians of the land.

Cherokee legends about the Nûñnë'hï often revolve around their interactions with humans. They are known to occasionally help or protect individuals, especially those who respect the land and the creatures of the mountains. However, they can also be mischievous and may lead travelers and hikers astray or play pranks on those who venture into their territory. Their stories reflect the deep connection between the Cherokee people and the landscape, emphasizing the importance of respecting

and coexisting with nature. The Nûñnë'hï, like other legendary beings in Cherokee folklore, have been documented by early European settlers in the region as well, and over time, these beings were synonymous with elves, gnomes, and fairies. This interaction between Native American legends and European settlers' accounts is an example of how these cultural influences intertwined in the development of the folklore.

Now that we've laid some groundwork, I invite you to keep these cultural elements in mind as you read my retelling of some of the most integral stories and superstitions from Appalachian folklore. Look for the Native American nature-spirit elements, seek out the mournful, wandering souls of Africa, and recognize the magic of the European forest sprites and lost soldiers. Notice how each story might be a caution, a curse, or a tale of a symbiotic relationship between a people, their landscape, and their ethics. Seek out the bridges between wildly different cultures that were able to come together and establish one of the most impactful and innovative cultures that have shaped modern America, as ageless and ancient as the very mountains that surround them.

SUPERSTITIONS, OMENS, AND SPOOKY TRADITIONS

Tucked beneath ancient forests and the hushed whispers of days gone by, Appalachia's communities hold a collection of superstitions, omens, and eerie traditions—enduring tales that have stood resilient against the march of time. Here, where the wind rustles the leaves and the land embraces its people, unfolds a distinctive cultural panorama, where the mystical coexists with the everyday. Rooted in a generational connection to the land, Appalachian people carry with them a silent guardianship of superstitions, warding against the unseen. From the hollows to the heights, stories echo across the rugged landscape—of spectral apparitions, elusive woodland spirits, and ominous omens—revealing a shared consciousness steeped in the unexplained. This chapter beckons a journey into the essence of these mountains, where lingering shadows and obscured mysteries shape the cultural landscape.

Prepare yourself to traverse the intricacies of Appalachian superstitions, where commonplace items morph into messengers and the line between the living and the spectral becomes as indistinct as mist weaving through time-worn summits. Through the lens of tradition, we will explore the ties that bind the living to the supernatural, diving into the folklore that animates the region's hills.

As we delve further, we'll discover a world where everyday beliefs profoundly influence the rhythm of daily life. In Appalachia, superstitions aren't merely relics of the past but living elements that shape a culture tightly bound to the mysteries of the unknown. Walk cautiously, for the spirits of Appalachia are watchful, and their stories patiently await their telling.

SUPERSTITIONS

Have you ever engaged in the ritual of knocking on wood or steering clear of walking beneath a ladder? Superstitions, it seems, have a way of sneaking into all our lives to some degree. However, in the heart of Appalachia, superstitions take on a unique and almost playful character. Nowadays, these superstitions are often uttered with a hint of humor. It's as if the folks in these mountains keep the traditions alive because their ancestors once did, and there's a lingering notion that, just maybe, there's a grain of truth in them.

Appalachian superstitions are a fascinating blend of old-world beliefs brought by early European settlers, the unique perspectives of African American folklore, and the enduring influence of Native American cultures that inhabited the region long before. These superstitions have become an integral part of Appalachian culture, guiding the daily lives of its people, uniting the cultures together within a shared community, and offering a glimpse into the deep-rooted traditions that shape the region. Here, we delve into the world of Appalachian superstitions, exploring their origins, significance, and enduring presence.

Here are some superstitions from Appalachian folklore:

- You should always go out the same door you came in. It's believed that using a different door can allow negative spirits or energies to enter, as it's considered a breach of the protective boundary established when entering through a specific doorway.

- Always carry a four-leaf clover to ward off bad luck. Each leaf of the four-leaf clover is traditionally believed to represent a different attribute: hope, faith, love, and luck. As a result, possessing a four-leaf clover is thought to bring positive energy and protect against negative influences.

- If a black cat crosses your path, draw an X in the air. This practice can be seen as a form of sympathetic magic, where a symbolic gesture is believed to influence events or outcomes.

- Eat black-eyed peas with greens and pork on New Year's Day for good luck. Black-eyed peas are often associated with luck and prosperity. Some believe that each pea represents a coin and consuming them on New Year's Day is thought to bring financial abundance in the coming year. Greens are associated with wealth and economic prosperity. Their green color is reminiscent of money, and the tradition suggests that the more greens you eat, the more wealth you'll accumulate in the new year. Pork is included in the New Year's Day meal for a couple of reasons. Pigs symbolize progress and forward movement because they root forward while foraging. Additionally, pork is considered a symbol of abundance and prosperity.

◆ Don't give knives as a wedding gift. This superstition is based on the idea that presenting a couple with a sharp object like a knife may bring bad luck or negatively impact their relationship. The symbolism behind this belief is often associated with the notion that sharp objects can cut ties, including the emotional bond between the newly-weds.

◆ When passing a cemetery, you had better hold your breath. The belief is that if you were to inhale while passing a cemetery, you could inhale the soul of a deceased person, which might attach itself to you. Some variations of this superstition suggest that inhaling the air near a cemetery could bring illness or misfortune. Holding one's breath is seen as a way to avoid exposure to potentially harmful spiritual energies.

◆ If a man wipes his hands on a woman's apron, he will fall in love with her. This superstition might have connections to folk magic or love spells. Throughout history, various cultures have employed rituals or actions to influence romantic outcomes, and the act of wiping hands on an apron could be seen as a simple form of sympathetic magic. The act of sharing an apron, even in a small and seemingly mundane way, creates a shared experience. It can symbolize a connection between the individuals involved, fostering a sense of intimacy and potential romantic interest.

- Pregnant women should avoid funerals because seeing a dead body will cause the baby to have a birthmark. Cultural beliefs often link the emotional state of the mother during pregnancy to potential outcomes for the child. Seeing a dead person may be considered a distressing or emotionally charged experience, and the superstition connects this emotional event to the formation of a birthmark on the baby.

- If you open a pocket knife, make sure you are the one to close it or you will have seven years of bad luck. Opening a knife may symbolize cutting through obstacles or severing ties, while closing it without having opened it could be interpreted as undoing or interrupting that action. This may be associated with a fear of reversing positive or protective measures.

HORSESHOES

Hanging a horseshoe over the doorway is believed to bring good luck and protect the home from evil spirits. The open end of the horseshoe typically faces upward or is wrapped in tin foil to catch and hold good luck. One might also carry a horseshoe nail for good luck on the go. You can place one in the fire to protect livestock, like sheep, from disease or wild animal attacks.

HAINTS AND SPIRITS

The most perennial Appalachian superstitions revolve around "haints," or restless spirits. To ward off these malevolent entities, many Appalachian homes, particularly those of the African American Gullah culture, are painted with a shade of blue known as "haint blue." It is believed that this color confuses and repels the spirits, preventing them from entering the house. Haint blue can often be seen on porch ceilings and window frames. Other common ghostly superstitions involve changing the doorknobs to your home after someone dies so that ghosts can't come in. Touching a dead person is another way to ensure that their spirit won't haunt you, but just remember not to sing or dance near your table, otherwise, you might not have any rest when you're dead and become the ghost doing the haunting.

MOON PHASES AND PLANTING

Appalachian farmers have long relied on the phases of the moon to guide their planting and harvesting. Planting during a waxing moon is thought to encourage growth while harvesting during a waning moon is believed to promote preservation. This practice reflects the deep connection between the agricultural rhythms of life and celestial phenomena.

CHARM PROTECTION

Appalachian culture places great importance on charms and talismans for protection against evil spirits, illness, or bad luck. These charms can range from simple items like a piece of iron, a horseshoe, or a particular coin, to more intricate arrangements involving herbs, minerals, or Bible verses. Placing these charms near entrances or wearing them as jewelry is believed to offer protection. The use of iron, for example, is rooted in a widespread belief that iron possesses inherent protective qualities against supernatural entities. Horseshoes, with their crescent shape, are thought to symbolize good luck and protection when hung over doorways or entrances. Similarly, certain coins may be chosen for their historical or cultural significance, believed to bring prosperity and safeguard against misfortune.

More intricate arrangements may involve a combination of items with specific properties. Herbs, chosen for their supposed medicinal or mystical qualities, are often incorporated into protective charms. Minerals, each believed to possess unique energies, are carefully selected to enhance the overall potency of the charm. Bible verses, chosen for their spiritual significance, are sometimes included to invoke divine protection.

The placement of these charms is crucial to their efficacy. Many individuals in the Appalachian region choose to hang or display these protective items near entrances, windows, or other vulnerable points in the home. Wearing them as jewelry, such as necklaces or bracelets, is another common practice, allowing individuals to carry their protective talismans with them wherever they go.

PROTECTION CHARM

Ingredients

A small piece of iron (such as a nail or horseshoe nail)

A small, square piece of cloth

Dried herbs for protective properties (e.g., rosemary, sage, or basil)

String or ribbon

Instructions

1 First, state aloud your intention for protection and safety. Then, take the piece of iron and hold it in your hands, envisioning a barrier around you.

2 Place the iron in the center of the cloth.

3 Add the dried herbs on top of the iron. Focus on the protective qualities of each herb. Imagine rosemary creating a shield of positive energy and repelling negativity. Visualize sage purifying your space and offering spiritual protection. Envision basil providing a layer of safety and dispelling harmful influences.

4 Gather the corners of the cloth and tie them together with the string or ribbon, creating a small pouch.

5 Hold the pouch in your hands and speak these words of protection or a simple prayer: "Guardian spirits, I ask for your protection. Surround me with your loving energy and keep me safe from all harm. May this charm serve as a shield against all danger. Amen."

PLANT SUPERSTITIONS

Appalachians have a profound connection to the land, and this is reflected in their plant-based superstitions. For example, it's believed that planting crops during certain moon phases can yield better results. Folk remedies using herbs and plants are also common for various ailments.

Sassafras

Known for its aromatic roots and distinctive sassafras leaves, this plant is often associated with spring tonics. It is believed that consuming tea made from sassafras roots in the spring can purify the blood and invigorate the body after the winter months. This practice aligns with the tradition of using seasonal plants for their perceived health benefits.

Ginseng

A medicinal herb native to the Appalachian forests, ginseng is highly valued for its purported health benefits. Harvesting ginseng is surrounded by superstitions, including the belief that disturbing the plant's environment or harvesting it at the wrong time can bring bad luck. Some harvesters adhere to specific rituals or avoid certain actions during the process to maintain the plant's potency.

Mullein

Recognized by its tall stalk and fuzzy leaves, mullein is often regarded as a protective herb. Hanging bundles of dried mullein near doorways or windows is thought to ward off evil spirits and negative energy, providing a sense of security to the household.

Black Walnut
Black walnut trees are considered protective in Appalachian superstitions. Placing black walnut branches or leaves around the home is believed to safeguard against malevolent forces. Additionally, nuts are sometimes used in rituals or charms for protection.

Elderberry
Elderberry bushes are associated with protection against illness. Some believe that planting elderberries near the home can prevent sickness, while others use elderberry-based remedies to ward off colds and flu. The folklore surrounding elderberries reflects a connection between plants and health in Appalachian culture.

FOLK HEALING PRACTICES

Appalachian folk often rely on traditional healing practices, such as granny magic or rootwork. These practices involve using herbs, minerals, and rituals to cure ailments or protect against curses.

The use of local plants and herbs for medicinal purposes is a cornerstone of Appalachian folk healing. Plants like ginseng, and elderberry are often employed to address various ailments. Folk healers in the Appalachians often consider the phases of the moon when performing healing rituals. Some believe that certain health-related activities, such as surgery or bloodletting, are more effective during specific lunar phases.

Some Appalachian folk-healing practices involve the casting or removal of spells to address ailments or protect individuals from harm. This may include rituals to ward off evil spirits or to bring about healing.

UNLUCKY DAYS

Friday the 13th

As in other cultures, Friday the 13th is considered an unlucky day in Appalachian superstition. It's a day when people may avoid starting new projects or making significant decisions. Some believe that the association of Friday the 13th with bad luck comes from Christian traditions. According to Christian beliefs, Friday was the day on which Jesus Christ was crucified. It is also said that Eve tempted Adam with the forbidden fruit on a Friday. The number 13 has historically been associated with betrayal in Christianity, as there were 13 individuals present at the Last Supper, including Judas Iscariot, who betrayed Jesus. The number 12 has historically been considered a "complete" or "perfect" number in various cultures. In contrast, the number 13 is seen as irregular or incomplete.

New Year's Day

In some Appalachian communities, starting certain activities on New Year's Day is believed to bring bad luck throughout the year. This superstition is rooted in the idea that the first day of the year sets the tone for the following months, and engaging in unlucky actions on this day may have lasting consequences. Washing clothes on New Year's Day could cause a death in the family. Sleeping on New Year's Day can lead to an unhappy year.

Leap Years

Leap years, and specifically February 29, are sometimes viewed with suspicion. Some superstitions suggest that activities initiated on this day may not prosper, and decisions made might lead to unfavorable outcomes. This belief likely stems from the irregularity of leap years, disrupting the usual calendar cycle.

First Monday in April

In some communities, the first Monday in April is considered an unlucky day for various activities, including starting new projects or planting crops. The reasons behind this superstition may be rooted in historical events or cultural practices associated with the beginning of spring.

May 1st

May 1 is considered unlucky in Appalachian folklore. Some associate this day with misfortune and caution against starting new projects or making major decisions. The superstition may be linked to historical events, changes in weather patterns, or ancient traditions associated with this date.

Last Monday in August

Like the superstition surrounding the first Monday in April, the last Monday in August is considered an inauspicious day for certain endeavors. This belief may be linked to agricultural practices or historical events influencing the community's outlook on this particular day.

ANIMAL SUPERSTITIONS

Animal superstitions in Appalachia, like in many other cultures, are rooted in a combination of historical, cultural, and practical influences. These superstitions often arise from observations of the natural world, a connection to the land, and a desire to make sense of the mysteries of life. Here are some examples of animal superstitions:

Black Cats

Similar to broader Western superstitions, a black cat crossing your path is often considered a bad omen. In some Appalachian communities, it's believed that this can bring bad luck or signal the presence of evil spirits.

Owls

Owls are associated with various superstitions. Some believe that hearing an owl hoot near a residence predicts a death in the family, while others view owls as messengers of wisdom and knowledge. Specifically, the hooting of a barred owl, known for it's distinctive call, is always considered a harbinger of bad news. The same can be said for screech owls, whose piercing calls forewarn of death.

Snakes

The presence of snakes is often considered a sign of danger or misfortune. Killing a snake is believed by some to bring bad luck, while others associate snakes with healing and transformation.

Crows

Crows and ravens are often associated with death or impending misfortune in Appalachian folklore. The number of crows seen together may be interpreted as a sign of the severity of the impending event. One crow can mean sorrow or bad news may be coming your way. Two crows can mean you'll have joy or good luck. Three crows can mean a wedding or celebration is coming. Four crows can signify a birth or major change. Five crows can mean sickness or poor health. Six crows can bring wealth or fortune. Seven crows can mean a secret or mystery. Eight crows can mean sadness or loss is coming your way. Nine crows can bring love or passion. Ten or more crows can mean a significant change or transformation is coming.

Groundhogs

The behavior of groundhogs, particularly on Groundhog Day, is believed to predict the weather. If a groundhog sees its shadow, it's thought to indicate six more weeks of winter, a tradition also common in various regions of the United States.

Cardinals

Some believe that seeing a red cardinal is a sign from a deceased loved one, bringing comfort and a message from the spirit world.

Crickets

Crickets are often considered good luck in Appalachian superstitions. Their chirping is believed to bring positive energy and is sometimes seen as a sign of good fortune.

Butterflies

Butterflies are associated with transformation and rebirth. Seeing a butterfly is often considered a positive sign, symbolizing the potential for personal growth or change.

Bats

Bats are sometimes associated with supernatural beliefs. In some Appalachian superstitions, the presence of bats is considered a sign of impending death or misfortune.

Robins

The arrival of robins in spring is often seen as a positive sign, symbolizing renewal and the end of winter. Some believe that seeing the first robin of the season brings good luck.

BROOM SUPERSTITIONS

Brooms hold a special place in Appalachian superstitions and represent a blend of practical beliefs, magical thinking, and cultural traditions. Here are some examples of broom superstitions:

- In Appalachian weddings, it's a tradition for the bride and groom to jump over a broom together. This act is believed to symbolize their entrance into a new phase of life and is thought to bring good luck, fertility, and domestic harmony. This tradition likely originated with enslaved Africans who, as domestic workers, used brooms often, to seal a matrimony.

- Placing a broom behind the door or leaning it against the wall was believed to ward off witches and evil spirits. This practice is rooted in historical superstitions about keeping witches from entering homes.

- There's a superstition that sweeping the house after dark invites bad luck. It was believed that sweeping at night might sweep away good fortune or attract negative energy.

- Sweeping dirt or dust directly out the front door was considered unlucky. It was believed to sweep away the household's prosperity and bring misfortune.

◆ If a broom falls while you are carrying it, it's thought to be a sign of visitors arriving soon. The number of drops may be associated with the number of visitors.

◆ Gifting a broom is considered bad luck unless the recipient gives a coin in return. This exchange is believed to prevent the relationship from being "swept away" and preserve good fortune.

◆ Some Appalachian households used brooms in rituals for protection. This might involve sweeping out negative energy or creating a barrier against evil spirits.

◆ There's a superstition that sweeping a single person's feet could prevent them from marrying. It was believed to "sweep away" their chances of finding a partner.

◆ In Appalachian folk magic, the broom has been used as a tool for protective spells. Brooms were sometimes hung over doorways or placed in specific areas to ward off evil and negative influences.

◆ Bringing a broom outside during a thunderstorm was considered dangerous. Folklore suggested that it could attract lightning or negative energy.

◆ Broom corn, a type of sorghum, was often used to make broom corn dolls. These dolls were believed to have protective qualities and were sometimes placed in homes to guard against evil spirits.

MIRROR SUPERSTITIONS

Mirror superstitions in Appalachian folklore, like in many other cultures, reflect a blend of practical beliefs, mystical thinking, and cultural traditions. Mirrors have long been associated with various superstitions and folklore, often tied to ideas about the soul, reflections, and the supernatural. Here are some mirror-related superstitions and beliefs in Appalachian folklore:

- Breaking a mirror is considered an omen of bad luck and is thought to bring seven years of misfortune. This superstition is rooted in the ancient belief that mirrors hold the reflections of the soul. Breaking one was seen as damaging a soul's connection to the body.

- Some Appalachian superstitions suggest covering mirrors during a thunderstorm. It is believed that the energy from the storm could enter the mirror and affect the well-being of those reflected in it.

- There's a belief that if you see a deceased person's reflection in a mirror, it is an omen or a sign that the spirit is present. This can be interpreted as a connection between the living and the spirit world.

- Covering mirrors at night is sometimes considered a protective measure. Leaving a mirror uncovered could allow spirits or supernatural entities to use the mirror as a portal.

- There's a superstition that breaking a mirror in a room brings bad luck to the entire household. Some variations suggest that breaking a mirror in a room where someone is ill can worsen the person's condition.

- Some beliefs caution against looking into mirrors at night. It is thought that doing so could call forth supernatural entities or attract negative energy.

- Mirrors were sometimes associated with the lunar cycle. Looking into a mirror during a full moon is believed to enhance divination abilities or reveal glimpses of the future.

- If you are pregnant and don't want to know the gender of your baby, avoid looking into a mirror at night, as some superstitions claim it could reveal the baby's gender or attract supernatural influences.

- Mirrors are sometimes used for protective purposes in Appalachian folk magic. Placing mirrors facing outward near doorways or windows was believed to reflect negative energy away from the home.

- Mirrors are sometimes employed in divination and spirit communication. It is believed that mirrors could be used as portals to connect with the spirit world.

- In some traditions, if a mirror breaks, the broken pieces are buried to prevent bad luck from affecting the household.

- There are also beliefs that mirrors can reveal the presence of illness or impending death. Seeing an ill or deceased person's reflection in a mirror could be interpreted as a forewarning.

COIN SUPERSTITIONS

Coins represent wealth and currency and carry symbolic value. In many cultures, including Appalachia, they symbolize prosperity, luck, and financial well-being. Superstitions involving coins often leverage these symbolic associations. Coins have historically been used in folk magic practices for their symbolic significance. Folk magic practitioners may incorporate coins into rituals, charms, or talismans believed to bring luck, protection, or other desired outcomes.

Coin Divination

Practitioners of folk magic in Appalachia may use coins as tools for divination. Tossing coins and interpreting their arrangement or the side facing up can provide insights into questions or concerns.

Offering Coins

Placing coins on certain objects or locations as an offering may be considered a way of seeking favor or protection. This practice is often tied to spiritual beliefs and may involve leaving coins at gravesites or sacred sites.

Found Coins

Superstitions related to coins abound in Appalachian folklore. For example, the belief that finding a coin on the ground brings good luck or that discovering a coin with a hole in it attracts prosperity.

Coin Charms

Carrying specific coins as charms or talismans is a practice rooted in superstition. Certain coins may be believed to bring protection, luck, or other positive influences when kept on one's person.

EVERYDAY SUPERSTITIONS

Some Appalachian superstitions are not as easy to categorize but are nonetheless frightening enough to abide by. Women are sure not to shower during the first few days of menstruation or they risk cramping to death! Another untimely death might be caused by rocking an empty rocking chair or putting your shoes on the bed.

It is a common belief that the body can carry signs and warnings of impending events. If your foot itches, it may be a sign of a long journey ahead. Have you ever heard the saying, "My nose itches, somebody is coming with a hole in their britches?" If your nose itches, it is a sign that company may be coming. If your ear is itching, someone is surely talking about you.

Superstitions about babies are ingrained in Appalachian folklore as well. Babies symbolize new beginnings and the continuation of life. Superstitions surrounding babies may reflect a cultural reverence for the cycles of life, and certain rituals or practices are believed to ensure a positive start for a newborn.

Choosing a baby's name is a significant decision. Some Appalachian superstitions suggest that it's important to keep the chosen name a secret until after the baby is born to protect the child from negative influences. Additionally, some superstitions caution against complimenting a baby's appearance too much. It is believed that too many compliments might attract envy or negative energy, potentially leading to harm.

Another superstition about babies is that you should wait until after the first birthday to cut the baby's hair. In Appalachian culture, it is believed that a baby's hair possesses protective qualities and cutting it prematurely may remove this protective energy.

OMENS

— · —

An omen is a belief or sign that is thought to predict or foreshadow future events, often carrying a sense of significance or warning. People interpret omens as messages from the supernatural, the natural world, or their own intuition. These signs can be positive or negative but are most commonly seen as a warning of an upcoming event. This means that they might foretell everything from bad weather and poor harvest to the presence of a deceased loved one. While we all have casual omens that we might notice (like 666 being a bad sign), in Appalachia, they are taken seriously and are strictly adhered to.

WEATHER OMENS

The Appalachian people have a long-held tradition of observing nature to predict weather patterns. Weather omens are observations and interpretations of natural phenomena believed to foretell specific weather conditions or events. Rooted in the region's agrarian history and a deep connection to the land, these omens often serve as practical indicators for agricultural planning and daily life. Here are some examples of weather omens in Appalachian folklore:

Red Sky at Night, Sailor's Delight; Red Sky in the Morning, Sailor's Warning
Meaning: A red sky at sunset is believed to indicate fair weather, while a red sky in the morning suggests an incoming storm. This saying reflects the idea that the color of the sky during sunrise or sunset can be predictive of weather patterns.

Ring around the Moon
Meaning: A ring or halo around the moon is often seen as a sign of approaching precipitation, typically rain or snow. The phenomenon is caused by the reflection, refraction, and dispersion of light through ice crystals in the atmosphere.

Woolly Bear Caterpillar
Meaning: The width of the brown and black bands on a Woolly Bear Caterpillar is thought to predict the severity of the upcoming winter. A wider brown band is believed to indicate a milder winter, while a narrower band suggests a harsher one.

Smoke from the Chimney
Meaning: The behavior of smoke rising from a chimney is observed to predict the weather. If the smoke rises straight up, it suggests fair weather, while if it swirls and descends, it may indicate an impending storm.

Rain on a Funeral
Meaning: Folklore suggests that rain during a funeral is a sign that the deceased has found peace and is now in a better place. This belief ties emotional events to natural occurrences.

Hooting Owls
Meaning: The hooting of owls is sometimes interpreted as a warning of bad weather or other negative events. The specific beliefs about owl calls can vary, with some associating them with storms or even death.

Cracking Corn bread
Meaning: The cracking or splitting of corn bread as it bakes is believed to indicate changes in the weather. For example, a crack down the middle of the loaf might signal an approaching storm.

Sun Dogs
Meaning: The appearance of bright spots on either side of the sun, known as sun dogs, is sometimes seen as a precursor to rainy weather.

These weather omens are often passed down through generations, with families and communities relying on these observations to plan their activities and make preparations for changing weather conditions.

ANIMAL OMENS

Animal omens have a special place in Appalachian folklore, where the behaviors and appearances of animals are often believed to foretell events, offer guidance, or carry symbolic meaning. These omens are deeply rooted in the connection between the natural world and the spiritual beliefs of the Appalachian people. Here are several animal omens and their interpretations in Appalachian folklore:

Black Cats
Similar to broader Western superstitions, in Appalachian folklore, if a black cat crosses your path from left to right, it is considered a particularly bad omen. This may signal impending bad luck or the presence of evil spirits. To counteract this bad luck, some believe you should take three steps backward or make the sign of the cross.

Butterflies
Butterflies are associated with transformation and renewal. Seeing a butterfly is often considered a positive sign, symbolizing the potential for personal growth or positive change.

Spiders
Finding a spider is often seen as a sign of good fortune, prosperity, and protection. Killing a spider, however, may bring bad luck.

Snakes
The presence of snakes is often considered a sign of danger or misfortune. Killing a snake is believed by some to bring bad luck, while others associate snakes with healing and transformation.

Bats
In some Appalachian superstitions, the presence of bats is considered a sign of impending death or misfortune.

BIRD OMENS

Birds, in particular, are associated with omens in Appalachian folklore. The call of certain birds, like the owl or the crow, is believed to foretell different events. The hoot of an owl at night can be seen as an omen of death, while a crow's call may signify the arrival of guests or a change in weather.

Here is a list of bird omens in Appalachian folklore:

Bird Behavior

The songs of birds are often interpreted as messages. Different birds and their songs may have specific meanings, and the timing or intensity of their singing could be seen as a good or bad omen. For example, the songs of birds are often interpreted as messages of good luck and positive energy so hearing them sing in the morning can be seen as a sign of a good day ahead or blessings to come. However, certain birds, like crows or owls, singing or calling near a home at night may be considered an omen of bad luck or an impending misfortune.

The flight patterns of birds, especially unusual behaviors, may be interpreted as signs. Birds flying low or in a certain direction might be considered good or bad omens. For example, birds flying high in the sky are generally seen as a sign of good fortune and clear weather ahead. If birds are flying towards you, it is often interpreted as good news or positive change coming your way. Birds flying low or erratically, especially towards the ground, can be seen as a bad omen, potentially signaling bad weather, illness, or other negative events. Birds flying away from you might be seen as a sign of missed opportunities or impending loss.

Specific Birds and Their Meanings

In many cultures, including Appalachia, owls are associated

with wisdom and mystery. Hearing the call of an owl is sometimes seen as a sign of upcoming changes or the need to pay attention to one's surroundings.

Crows and Ravens are often associated with intelligence and foresight. Seeing a crow or raven may be interpreted as a message about the future, and their behavior may indicate potential challenges or opportunities.

Cardinals are often associated with positive energy and spiritual messages. Some believe that the presence of a cardinal is a sign that a departed loved one is watching over the living.

Migration Patterns
Bird migration patterns are observed as omens, especially in relation to changing seasons. The timing of migrations may be seen as an indicator of weather changes or events.

Feather Omens
The discovery of feathers, especially in unexpected places, may be seen as a sign of guidance or protection. The color and size of the feather could influence the interpretation. For instance, white feathers are often regarded as symbols of purity, peace, and protection. They are commonly interpreted as messages from guardian angels or deceased loved ones, suggesting that these spiritual beings are watching over you. In contrast, black feathers are typically linked to protection and caution. They may indicate a need for vigilance or serve as a reminder to take care of oneself.

Nesting and Building Behaviors
The way birds build their nests or choose nesting locations might be interpreted as symbolic. For example, a bird building a nest near a home could be seen as a positive omen.

Divination through Birds

Some traditions involve divination through birds. The interpretation of a bird's behavior or the presence of certain birds in specific situations may provide insights into future events or decisions. Seeing doves might be interpreted as a positive sign, symbolizing peace and prosperity, and could indicate that the choice you are considering will bring harmony and success. In contrast, encountering crows or ravens may be seen as a warning. If these birds are cawing loudly or flying erratically, it could suggest potential challenges or obstacles ahead.

Weather Predictions

Birds are often observed for indications of upcoming weather changes. Changes in feeding patterns, vocalizations, or gathering behaviors may be interpreted as signs of changing atmospheric conditions.

Communication with the Spirit World

Birds are sometimes viewed as messengers between the earthly realm and the spirit world. Their appearance or behavior may be considered a form of communication from ancestors or other spiritual entities.

DREAM OMENS

Dream omens are interpretations of dreams that are believed to provide insights into future events, offer guidance, or convey messages from the spiritual realm. These dream interpretations reflect the cultural and spiritual beliefs of the Appalachian people. Here are some examples of Appalachian dream omens:

Flying Dreams

Dreams of flying are often seen as positive omens. They may indicate personal freedom, overcoming obstacles, or achieving success. Flying dreams might suggest a sense of empowerment and the ability to rise above challenges.

Snake Dreams

Snakes are powerful symbols in many cultures. In Appalachian folklore, dreaming of snakes may signify transformation, healing, or the need for caution. The specific context of the dream, such as the snake's behavior, color, or actions, is often considered in the interpretation.

Teeth Falling Out

Dreaming of teeth falling out is a common theme with various interpretations. In Appalachian folklore, it might be seen as a sign of change, transition, or a need to pay attention to one's health. The dreamer's age and personal circumstances may influence the interpretation.

Water Dreams

Dreams involving water, such as rivers, lakes, or oceans, are believed to carry different meanings. Clear or calm water might represent tranquility, while murky or turbulent water could signify challenges or emotional turmoil. The presence of water in a dream likely carries a spiritual message. The specific actions in the dream, like swimming or drowning, also contribute to the interpretation.

Animal Dreams

Dreams featuring animals are thought to convey messages or warnings. For example, encountering a bear in a dream might symbolize strength and protection while a fox could represent cunning or deception.

Death Dreams

Dreaming of a deceased loved one is often seen as a connection to the spiritual realm. In Appalachia, these dreams might be interpreted as messages or visitations from the departed or ancestors. The emotions experienced during the dream are considered important for understanding the message.

White Clothes
Dreams involving the wearing of white clothes are believed to signify purity, spiritual growth, or positive changes. The presence of white animals or objects in the dream might reinforce these positive interpretations.

Storm Dreams
Dreams featuring storms, thunder, or lightning are often associated with powerful forces and changes. Depending on the dream's context, storms may symbolize cleansing, renewal, or emotional upheaval.

PLANT OMENS

Plant omens in Appalachian folklore involve the interpretation of the behavior, growth patterns, or occurrences related to plants as signs or messages. Rooted in a deep connection to nature, these omens are often influenced by a blend of Indigenous, European, and African traditions.

The presence and behavior of certain plants, such as Jack-in-the-Pulpit, are sometimes interpreted as omens in Appalachian superstitions. For instance, if Jack-in-the-Pulpit is open wide, it is believed to indicate good weather, while a closed appearance may suggest rain.

Here are some key aspects of plant omens in Appalachian folklore:

Blooming and Flowering
The timing and abundance of blooms on plants are often interpreted as omens. An unusually early or late flowering might

be seen as a sign of upcoming weather changes or shifts in the natural environment.

Plant Growth and Vigor

The overall health and vigor of plants may be observed for omens. Lush and vibrant growth is often considered a positive sign, while wilting or stunted growth might be interpreted as an indicator of challenges.

Unusual Plant Occurrences

Unusual or unexpected occurrences related to plants, such as a plants flowering out of season, may be seen as omens. These occurrences are believed to carry messages about the natural balance or potential disruptions in the environment.

Plant Associations in Folk Medicine

The use of plants in folk medicine is closely tied to omens. The growth, abundance, or scarcity of specific medicinal plants might be interpreted as indicators of health or illness within the community.

Herbal Folklore

The properties and folklore associated with specific herbs contribute to plant omens. For example, the belief that certain herbs have protective qualities might lead to interpretations based on their presence or absence in a particular area.

Poisonous Plants and Warnings

The presence of poisonous plants or fungi may be interpreted as a warning or omen. Observing an abundance of toxic plants in an area might be seen as a sign to exercise caution, not only in that area but in life in general.

Plant Communication

Some Appalachian traditions involve the belief that plants can communicate messages. This communication may occur through the rustling of leaves, the direction in which plants lean, or other subtle movements interpreted as responses to questions or concerns.

Plant Divination

Divination practices involving plants, such as reading the shapes of leaves or patterns in plant growth, are employed to gain insights into the future or receive guidance. These practices are often passed down through families.

Dreaming of Plants

Dreams featuring plants or specific plant-related scenarios may be interpreted as omens. The emotions and context of the dream contribute to the overall interpretation, guiding individuals in their decision-making.

Seasonal Changes

Observing changes in plant behavior across seasons is integral to Appalachian plant omens. The timing of leaf fall, bud emergence, or the appearance of certain plants may be associated with specific events or conditions.

Environmental Harmony

Plant omens are often seen as reflections of the overall harmony or imbalance in the natural environment. The interplay between different plant species and their relationships with other elements of nature is carefully observed for signs of balance or disruption.

Appalachian plant omens are part of a broader cultural and spiritual connection to the natural world.

NUMBER OMENS

In Appalachian numerology folklore, certain numbers are believed to carry specific meanings and significance. These interpretations often draw from a combination of cultural, religious, and mystical influences.

3

Meaning: Unity, Harmony, Completion.

Significance: The number three is often associated with completeness and harmony. In Christian traditions, it can represent the Holy Trinity.

4

Meaning: Stability, Foundation.

Significance: The number four is often associated with stability and a solid foundation. It represents balance and the four elements.

6

Meaning: Harmony, Family.

Significance: Linked to harmony and balance, the number six is also associated with familial relationships and community.

7

Meaning: Spiritual Perfection, Completeness.

Significance: Considered a sacred and powerful number, seven is associated with spiritual completeness. It often appears in biblical contexts and is seen as auspicious.

8

Meaning: Prosperity, Infinity.

Significance: The number eight is linked to prosperity and infinity. It is seen as a symbol of abundance and the cyclical nature of life.

9

Meaning: Culmination, Endings, Transition.

Significance: The number nine is linked to endings and transitions. It can signify the completion of a cycle, preparing for a new beginning.

11

Meaning: Spiritual Insight, Intuition.

Significance: Considered a master number in numerology, eleven is associated with spiritual insight and intuition. It is often seen as a connection to higher realms.

13

Meaning: Controversial, Transformation.

Significance: While often considered unlucky in Western superstition, the number thirteen can also represent transformation and change. In some contexts, it is associated with overcoming obstacles.

22

Meaning: Master Builder, Manifestation.

Significance: Another master number, twenty-two is associated with being a master builder, capable of turning dreams into reality through focused effort.

These interpretations are generalizations, and individual beliefs may vary. In Appalachian folklore, the meanings assigned to numbers often have roots in cultural traditions, religious beliefs, and a holistic understanding of the interconnectedness of nature and spirituality. Numerology in this context is part of a broader system of divination and interpretation that enriches the tapestry of the region.

COIN OMENS

Finding a coin, particularly a penny, is often seen as a symbol of good luck. Some believe that finding a coin with the year of one's birth can bring extra luck. Coin omens in Appalachian folklore involve the interpretation of the appearance, location, or circumstances surrounding coins as signs or messages. Here are some key aspects of coin omens in Appalachian folklore:

Finding Coins
Finding a coin, especially in an unexpected or unusual location, is often seen as a positive omen. It may be interpreted as a sign of good luck, financial blessings, or a positive turn of events.

Specific Coins
The type of coin found may carry additional significance. For example, finding a silver coin might be associated with purity while finding a gold coin could symbolize wealth and prosperity.

Direction and Placement
The direction in which a coin is facing, or its placement, may be considered in the interpretation. Some believe that a coin facing heads up brings good luck, while a coin facing tails up may indicate challenges or caution.

Gifts of Coins

Receiving coins as gifts, especially from someone with good intentions, may be seen as a positive sign. The act of giving coins symbolizes generosity and goodwill.

Coin-tossing Rituals

Coin-tossing rituals, where a coin is flipped and the outcome is interpreted, may be employed for decision-making, or seeking guidance. Which side is facing up or the way the coin lands is believed to convey a message.

Historical Context

The historical context of coins, especially older or rare coins, may contribute to their interpretation. For example, finding a coin from a specific era might be associated with messages from the past.

MIRROR OMENS

Breaking a mirror is widely believed to bring seven years of bad luck, a superstition shared with many other cultures. Some also cover mirrors during thunderstorms to protect against lightning strikes. Mirror omens in Appalachian folklore involve the interpretation of events, symbols, or visions reflected in mirrors as signs or messages. These omens support the belief in the mystical qualities of mirrors and the potential for glimpses into the spiritual or supernatural realm. Here are some key aspects of mirror omens in Appalachian folklore:

Mirror Divination

Mirrors are sometimes used as tools for divination. Practitioners may gaze into the mirror, often in a dimly lit room, to receive insights into the future, communicate with spirits, or gain a deeper understanding of their own psyche.

Veiling and Unveiling

The act of covering or uncovering a mirror may be associated with protection or the unveiling of hidden truths. Some believe that covering mirrors at night prevents spirits from entering or leaving through the reflective surface.

Broken Mirrors

Breaking a mirror is often considered an omen of bad luck in Western superstition, including in Appalachia. Some believe that breaking a mirror can shatter the soul's reflection, leading to misfortune or spiritual disturbances.

Reflection of the Deceased

Seeing the reflection of a deceased person in a mirror may be interpreted as a visitation or message from the spirit world. This can be both comforting and eerie, depending on the individual's beliefs.

Mirror Charms and Amulets

Mirrors are sometimes incorporated into charms or amulets for protection against negative entities or the evil eye. Hanging small mirrors near entrances or windows is believed to deflect negative energy.

Avoiding Mirrors at Night

Some superstitions advise against looking into mirrors at night, especially by candlelight. It is believed that mirrors may reveal otherworldly entities or supernatural occurrences during the nighttime.

Mirrors as Portals
In certain beliefs, mirrors are considered portals to other dimensions or realms. Staring into a mirror for an extended period may be seen as an invitation for spiritual communication or the unveiling of hidden knowledge.

Mirror Visions
Gazing into a mirror with a receptive mindset may lead to visions, symbols, or messages. Individuals may interpret these visions subjectively, seeking guidance or insights into their own lives.

Scrying Mirrors
Some mirrors are specifically designed for scrying, a form of divination. Scrying mirrors are often dark or black, and practitioners may use them to receive messages from the spirit world or gain intuitive insights.

Historical Context
The historical context of mirrors, especially antique or heirloom mirrors, may contribute to their significance. Mirrors passed down through generations may be regarded as conduits for ancestral connections.

SPOOKY TRADITIONS

The Appalachian region, with its rugged landscapes and diverse cultural heritage, is home to a variety of spooky traditions and customs. Yet, at the core of these traditions is the art of storytelling. Passed down through oral traditions, these tales serve as a living testament to the region's history, beliefs, and the collective consciousness of its people. In the flickering glow of fireside gatherings, stories come alive, painting vivid images of the supernatural and breathing life into the myths that have endured the passage of time.

These traditions also act as a bridge between the known and the unknown, helping the people of Appalachia navigate life's uncertainties. In the narrow, secluded valleys known as hollers, as well as the surrounding highlands, superstitions, omens, signs, and traditions serve as silent sentinels, offering protection against the unseen. Everyday objects become messengers, and the line between the living and the spectral blurs like the fog weaving through ancient peaks.

These spooky traditions are an integral part of Appalachian culture, reflecting the region's complex history, its reliance on storytelling, and its enduring connection to the supernatural. Whether as a form of entertainment or as a way to navigate life's mysteries, these traditions continue to thrive in the Appalachian region.

GHOST STORIES

It seems as if Appalachians have always told stories of ghosts roaming and haunting their lands. These tales often feature restless spirits, haunted houses, and eerie encounters in the wilderness. Storytellers gather around campfires or in dimly lit cabins to share these spine-tingling narratives, often accompanied by the sounds of howling winds and rustling leaves.

GRAVEYARD CUSTOMS

Appalachian cemeteries are often the setting for spooky traditions. Some people believe that you should never count the graves in a cemetery, as it might summon the spirits. It's also customary to leave offerings like coins, flowers, or small trinkets on the graves of loved ones to honor and appease their spirits.

JACK TALES

Jack tales are a genre of Appalachian storytelling that often involve a clever protagonist named Jack who outsmarts supernatural beings or villains. These tales blend humor with the supernatural, and they are often passed down from generation to generation. These are fairy tales, of sorts, and are likely the product of European fairy lore (known as Märchen) intermingling with the other cultures that make up the region's population.

DIVINATION AND FOLK MAGIC

Appalachian traditions include various forms of divination and folk magic. Methods such as reading tea leaves, dowsing for water, or using pendulums to answer questions are practiced by some as ways to gain insight into the future or make decisions.

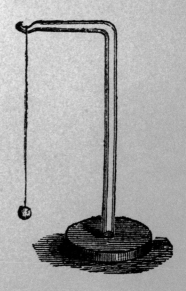

APPARITIONS AND HAINTS

In the hidden enclaves and mist-draped corners of Appalachia, where the ancient mountains guard their secrets with whispered tales, lies a realm where the spirits of the past roam free. This chapter invites you to step into the ethereal world of Appalachian apparitions and haints, where the veil between the living and the dead is thin, and the echoes of bygone souls linger like a haunting melody on the wind. Here, amid the rugged terrain and deep-rooted traditions, haintly encounters are woven into the very fabric of Appalachian life. From the phantom lights that dance along remote mountain paths to the spectral figures that glide through moonlit clearings, each encounter offers a glimpse into a realm beyond the tangible, where the echoes of history reverberate through the ages.

APPARITIONS

Reported accounts of brushes with ghostly apparitions are not mere tales spun from the mists of imagination; they are the echoes of real encounters, passed down through generations with the weight of truth. In the forgotten corners of Appalachian homesteads and the crumbling ruins of once-vibrant communities, the apparitions of the past linger, their presence palpable in the chill of the night air and the whispers of the ancient trees. Through these encounters, we glimpse not only the shadows of the past but also the resilience of the human spirit in the face of the unknown. From the restless souls seeking peace in the afterlife, to the benevolent spirits guiding lost travelers home, the apparitions of Appalachia offer a haunting testament to the enduring power of human connection, even beyond the veil of death.

THE GHOSTS OF SENECA LAKE

At the end of the last ice age, over one hundred thousand years ago, massive glaciers advanced southward from Canada, carving deep trenches into the earth. As the earth warmed and the glaciers receded, the trenches filled with water and formed what we now know as the Finger Lakes. Seneca Lake, the largest of these, holds not only natural beauty but also a wealth of ghostly tales that have woven themselves into the fabric of local folklore.

Perched on the northwest shore of Seneca Lake, Belhurst Castle stands as a testament to grandeur and mystery. The castle, built in the late 19th century, is not only an architectural marvel but also a hotspot for ghostly activity. The most famous of its spectral residents is Isabella, a beautiful opera singer who fled Europe with her lover, the Spanish Don.

Isabella and her lover built a secret tunnel leading to the lake, a passage meant to provide a swift escape from any potential danger. Unfortunately, their love story met a tragic end. One night, as they attempted to flee through the tunnel, it collapsed, burying Isabella alive. Her lover, unable to save her, watched helplessly as the earth swallowed her. The legend says Isabella's anguished spirit never left the grounds of Belhurst Castle.

But Belhurst Castle is not the only place around Seneca Lake shrouded in eerie tales. The lake itself is said to be haunted by mysterious apparitions and unexplained phenomena. Locals speak of the "Lady in the Lake," a spectral figure seen gliding over the water on misty nights. According to legend, she is the ghost of a young woman who drowned in the lake long ago, her spirit eternally searching for peace.

Fishermen and boaters on Seneca Lake have reported strange occurrences, such as sudden, unexplained drops in temperature and ghostly voices carried in the wind. Some even claim to have seen ghostly ships sailing across the lake— their origins unknown and their destinations a mystery. These spectral vessels are said to appear and vanish without a trace, leaving behind only the whispers of their haunting journeys.

The haunted wineries along Seneca Lake add another layer to the area's paranormal reputation. At various historic wineries, staff and visitors have recounted numerous unexplained occurrences: flickering lights, sudden cold drafts, and the feeling of being watched. Objects move on their own, doors open and close with no apparent cause, and soft whispers can be heard in the dead of night. The spirits of former owners and workers are believed to linger, their presence felt in the very walls of these aged buildings.

THE PHANTOM HITCHHIKER OF ROUTE 44

In the shadowy depths of the Appalachian night, a chilling legend has woven itself into the very fabric of Route 44—an eerie tale of the Phantom Hitchhiker that has sent shivers down the spines of those who dare to traverse this desolate road.

It was on a moonless night, when the air itself held its breath, that a weary traveler found themselves on Route 44. The road, a serpentine path through remote wilderness, seemed to wind endlessly into the heart of the unknown. The only companions were the rhythmic hum of the engine and the oppressive darkness that enveloped the vehicle.

As the car pressed onward through the inky blackness, a shadowy figure emerged from the depths of the night. A hitchhiker, spectral and elusive, appeared on the roadside as if conjured from the very ether. It was a young woman with raven-black hair cascading like a waterfall of shadows, her thumb outstretched, beckoning for a ride.

Driven by compassion and an unspoken obligation, the driver slowed their car and pulled over to offer the mysterious traveler a lift. The young woman, a specter of ethereal beauty, glided into the back seat without a word. Her voice, when she finally spoke, was a haunting melody that echoed through the vehicle like a ghostly refrain.

"Thank you for stopping," she murmured softly, her words laden with a disconcerting allure. "I've waited an eternity for a ride."

The driver, their unease growing like ivy in their chest, nodded and continued the journey. Conversation, though polite, twisted into a macabre dance of tales from a distant town and a long-lost home.

As the miles unfurled like the fabric of darkness, the young woman's demeanor shifted, her aura of friendliness eroded by the weight of her melancholy. She began to recount a story—a tragic tale of an accident that had claimed her life on Route 44 many years ago. Her voice quivered with sorrow, her eyes drowning in pools of grief.

But before the driver could react, fate intervened. The car hurtled toward a treacherous bend in the road, and in a glance at the rearview mirror, the driver's heart ceased its steady rhythm. The young woman, the spectral hitchhiker, had vanished into thin air, leaving behind only an icy, lingering chill.

Terror clutched at the driver's chest, and they veered the car to a halt. Panic set in as they scoured the area, desperately seeking the vanished passenger. The night remained still, and the road, once a passage of escape, had become a realm of surreal solitude.

Confusion and dread in tow, the driver continued down Route 44, haunted by the inexplicable encounter. It wasn't until they reached a nearby town and inquired about the mysterious young woman that the shrouded truth was revealed.

The girl, they discovered, was not among the living. She was the ghost of a young girl who had met her tragic end in a car accident on Route 44 many years ago. Her spirit, forever tethered to the road, wandered in search of solace, redemption, or perhaps just a fleeting connection with the world of the living.

THE GHOSTLY SOLDIERS OF GETTYSBURG

A tale of restless spirits that still roam the historic battlegrounds of Gettysburg, this is a story that's whispered in hushed tones around campfires, a legend of ghostly soldiers who refuse to let go of their turbulent past.

Many years ago, in the midst of the American Civil War, the small town of Gettysburg, Pennsylvania, found itself thrust into the heart of a conflict that would change the course of history. It was a battle that raged for three long days, a brutal and blood-soaked struggle between the Union and Confederate forces, each vying for a grip on what is now known as the United States of America.

As the sun set on that final day of battle, the fields were littered with the fallen—brave soldiers who had given their lives for a cause they held dear. The cries of agony, the thunder of cannons, and the stench of death hung heavy in the air, as did the mist that stretched across the land and floated above the trenches.

As the smoke began to clear after the last crack of gunfire, a somber silence descended upon Gettysburg. The town had become a makeshift hospital, a place where the wounded were tended to on blood-stained stretchers and the dead were laid to rest beneath the fertile ground. But amid the quiet, something else lingered—a spine-tingling presence, an almost tangible spectral reminder of the horrors that had unfolded.

In the years that followed, countless reports have surfaced of ghostly apparitions and eerie phenomena on and around the Gettysburg battlefield. It is said that the restless spirits of fallen

soldiers still walk the earth, forever trapped in the memories of that fateful battle.

One chilling tale tells of a group of visitors who, not too long ago while exploring the battlefield at night, witnessed a phantom regiment of soldiers marching in formation. Their ghostly figures were clad in tattered uniforms, their eyes hollow and distant, their wounds gaping and raw, still seeping blood. The sound of their spectral boots hitting the ground echoed through the night as if they were reenacting a march from long ago. As one terrifying soldier broke formation and turned a wicked, yet almost pleading stare their way, the group ran out of there as quickly as they could, only to recount their terrifying ordeal around campfires and at play parties.

An especially haunted area in Northern Appalachia is Little Round Top, the smaller of two rocky hills that are just south of the Gettysburg battlefield. On July 2, 1863, Confederate soldiers launched a particularly brutal assault on the Union army's left flank. Unexpected and swift, Confederate soldiers were certain they were poised to overtake their enemy and emerge victorious. However, the exact opposite happened: The Union soldiers were prepared and not only held off the blitz but they also ultimately and ferociously rose up and conquered their invaders in a battle so bloody and savage that even the history books shudder to recount the tale.

Many Confederate shadows still haunt Little Round Top to this day, but visitors to the region report seeing the same, singular soldier wandering the hills, seemingly searching for his home. . . or his grave. The figure has been seen gazing out across the battlefield; his gaze fixed on a distant point. Witnesses claim that he appears so lifelike that he is often mistaken for a living reenactor. But as they draw closer, hoping to strike up a conversation, the shape of him begins to slowly dissolve into smoke that swirls and then vanishes into thin air.

But perhaps the most haunting of all are the reports of phantom wails and whispered voices heard on the battlefield. Some visitors speak of feeling an overwhelming sense of sadness and despair as they wander through the fields, as though the anguish of those who perished there is a living, breathing entity of its own. Over the years, Gettysburg has become known as one of the most haunted places in America, a place where the echoes of the past refuse to fade away. The ghostly soldiers, forever trapped in their spectral reenactment of battle, serve as a poignant reminder of the sacrifices made during those dark days of the Civil War.

THE WHITE LADY OF WHITE HALL

Nestled in the heart of Kentucky, there lies a grand plantation known as White Hall. Once a place of wealth and prosperity, it was the home of the Cassius Marcellus Clay family—a prominent name in the annals of American history. But behind the grandeur and opulence of the mansion, a tragic tale of love and loss would be etched into the very walls of White Hall.

The story begins with the vivacious and charming Cassius Marcellus Clay, Jr., a dashing young man with a thirst for adventure. He was known for his fiery spirit and his unwavering dedication to his beliefs. But Cassius was not alone in his pursuit of justice; he was joined by a radiant young woman named Mary Jane Warfield.

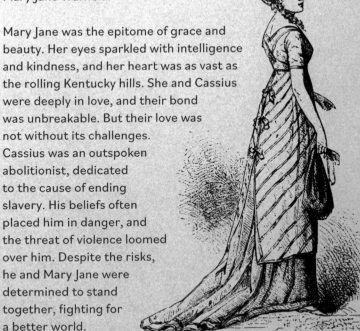

Mary Jane was the epitome of grace and beauty. Her eyes sparkled with intelligence and kindness, and her heart was as vast as the rolling Kentucky hills. She and Cassius were deeply in love, and their bond was unbreakable. But their love was not without its challenges. Cassius was an outspoken abolitionist, dedicated to the cause of ending slavery. His beliefs often placed him in danger, and the threat of violence loomed over him. Despite the risks, he and Mary Jane were determined to stand together, fighting for a better world.

One fateful night, as they sat on the porch of White Hall, a group of pro-slavery vigilantes descended upon the plantation. They were determined to silence Cassius and his passionate speeches. In the chaos that ensued, Cassius was severely beaten, and Mary Jane was kidnapped.

Cassius survived the attack but was left forever scarred, both physically and emotionally. He spent the rest of his life searching for Mary Jane, but she was never found. Her disappearance remained a haunting mystery, one that cast a dark shadow over the once happy estate.

In the years that followed, those who visited White Hall claimed to have encountered an apparition of a lady in white. She would appear in the moonlight, her ethereal form moving gracefully through the gardens and along the pathways. Her eyes were filled with sadness, and her outstretched arms seemed to reach out in search of something—or someone.

Some said that the White Lady is the ghost of Mary Jane, forever searching for her lost love, Cassius. Others believe that she is a symbol of the enduring love and tragedy that had unfolded at White Hall.

THE PHANTOM TRAIN OF BUCKS COUNTY

Buck's County, Pennsylvania, is known for many things: It's the point where George Washington's army crossed the Delaware River in a famed attack during the Revolutionary War, it's the home of William Penn's sweeping historical estate, and it houses many wartime museums that tell the stories of vicious wars and stately battle strategy. But only the luckless few know firsthand of the frightening apparitional train that haunts the locals throughout the year. These are stories that are told around the hearth and whispered at bedtime, stories about a ghostlike train that emerges from the shadows, rolling along the forgotten tracks of the past.

The legend centers around the long-abandoned rail lines that once connected small towns and communities across Bucks County, enabling the trade of goods and ensuring the transportation of workers to locations for much-needed work. According to the lore, a tragic event unfolded many years ago, leading to the demise of a train and its passengers. The specifics of the incident vary in different versions of the story, but a common thread involves a catastrophic derailment, claiming the lives of those aboard.

As the legend goes, the ghostly train reenacts its final, fateful journey on certain moonlit nights. Witnesses speak of hearing phantom whistles, the clatter of wheels on the tracks, and the distant echo of long-forgotten steam engines. Some claim to have seen ethereal lights moving through the darkness, a spirit-like reminder of the train that met its tragic fate.

Locals often caution against venturing too close to the abandoned tracks during these eerie nights. The air reportedly becomes thick with otherworldly energy, and those who have witnessed the spectral train describe an overwhelming sense of sadness and despair. While skeptics dismiss the tale as mere folklore, others embrace it as a haunting reminder of the region's history.

Among a plethora of warnings about the ghost train are nestled first-hand accounts of travelers and residents reporting other happenings along the tracks, like seeing whisps of ancient spirits and hearing nearly human-sounding howling winds. One such example is that of the Spirit Wolf of Solebury Hill. Timber wolves were said to roam freely during colonial times, often in great, formidable packs, hunting the land and rearing their young. It is said that a hunter in the in the early 1800s trapped the last of this majestic and fierce species, and that their kind was lost forever. However, a large ghost wolf has been seen by brave adventurers along the New Hope and Ivyland Railroad between Buckingham and Solebury, although none of these ghost-hunting pilgrims have stuck around long enough to find out what kind of damage this creature can do.

THE GHOST SHIP
OF LAKE ONTARIO

Nestled between the Canadian province of Ontario and the great state of New York is Lake Ontario. For some, this is a place of recuperation after a long work week, where one might go to blow off some steam, picnic with their family, or take the boat out for a spin. To others, this is a harrowing place full of terrifying mystery and unexplained events. One such legend is the Ghost Ship of Lake Ontario, a haunting tale that has captured the imaginations of those living along the shores of this great lake.

As the locals tell it, a mysterious and spectral ship appears during stormy nights, sailing the turbulent waters as if untouched by the tempest. According to witnesses, the Ghost Ship is an eerie reminder of a tragic event that unfolded many years ago. Some versions of the tale attribute the spectral vessel to a ship that sank in a fierce storm, claiming the lives of its crew and passengers. Others suggest that the ship is a phantom mirage, a manifestation of the lake's unpredictable and treacherous nature.

Those who claim to have seen the Ghost Ship describe it as a ghostly apparition, illuminated by a supernatural light that cuts through the darkness, on a voyage to seemingly nowhere. The ship is said to glide silently across the water, defying the storm's wrath and appearing almost translucent in the moonlight.

Legend has it that those who catch a glimpse of the Ghost Ship may witness the figures of sailors on its deck, eternally reenacting their final moments before succumbing to the cold embrace of Lake Ontario. The sounds of haunted voices and phantom footsteps allegedly echo across the water, carried by the wind as a searing reminder of the ship's tragic fate.

Many stories surround the unearthly vessel, each adding its own spin to the terrifying tale. Some speak of ghostly hands reaching out from the water, while others claim that the ship occasionally disappears into thin air, leaving nothing but ripples on the lake's surface, a tuft of fog lingering in its place.

THE CURSE OF DUDLEYTOWN

Dudleytown, Connecticut, also known as the Village of the Damned, is a notorious and allegedly cursed ghost town located adjacent to Cornwall. The legend of Dudleytown dates back to the eighteenth century and has become one of the most enduring and chilling tales of supernatural occurrences in all of New England.

According to the legend, the original Dudleytown curse was brought to the region by the Dudley family, descendants of Edmund Dudley, an Englishman who was beheaded for treason during the reign of King Henry VII, and with whom the curse is believed to originate. The Dudley family migrated and established the village in a secluded and densely wooded area, and over the years the town grew and began to thrive. But the sleeping curse awoke, and the village was plagued by a series of serious, fatal misfortunes.

The unfortunate events included unexplained and untimely (sometimes violent) deaths, insanity, crop failure, starvation,

disease, and strange occurrences. Residents of Dudleytown were said to inherit the curse with each generation, with none left unscathed. Staunch warnings were offered to those who newly settled in the village and faced unimaginable tragedies themselves, left wishing they had heeded their neighbors' alarms. Some stories spoke of residents losing their minds, strolling naked in the chill of a winter's night, or pulling out their hair with a chilling grin and locked stare, while others suggested that dark entities and demons lurked in the woods surrounding the township.

The fables surrounding Dudleytown intensified as the village began to decline, with residents leaving and the farmland falling into disrepair. By the mid-nineteenth century, Dudleytown had all but vanished, leaving behind only scattered remnants and memories of its eerie history.

Over the years, Dudleytown gained a reputation as one of the most haunted places in Connecticut. Numerous paranormal investigators and enthusiasts have reported strange phenomena in the area, including unexplained noises, ghostly apparitions, and feelings of deep unease. However, it's worth noting that no historical evidence supports the existence of a curse or supernatural events in Dudleytown, but one thing is for certain: you can either listen to the history books, or you can listen to what the people who lived through it all say, and I, for one, know exactly which camp I fall under.

THE BLACK DOG OF HANGING HILLS

The Black Dog of Hanging Hills is a daunting and frightful apparition associated with the Hanging Hills region in Connecticut, a subrange of the Appalachian Mountains. The sighting of an astonishingly large, ghostly black dog is often considered a forewarning of doom, appearing to unsuspecting locals, and visiting hikers as a shadowy canine with fiery red eyes. Its presence is said to be an omen, foretelling misfortune or tragedy to those who are unfortunate enough to encounter it. With deep roots in regional folklore, the origin of the legend is uncertain, as tales of spectral black dogs are common in various cultures around the world. While the surrounding communities are made up of an eclectic mishmash of peoples and cultures, in nearly all cases, these types of apparitions are associated with death or supernatural occurrences. The Hanging Hills version of the legend has become a part of the rich tapestry of Connecticut's folklore and a defining feature of its unique communities.

Some stories describe the Black Dog as a benevolent figure, guiding lost travelers safely through the treacherous terrain of the Hanging Hills. However, the prevailing belief is that encountering the Black Dog is a sign of tragedy to come, with some accounts linking its appearance to fatal accidents or other calamities.

HAINTS

The term "haint" was originally coined in the Carolina coast but has since become a term for a certain type of ghost or spirit in the southern region of the Appalachians. The term, and the belief in haints, was likely started by the Gulla Geechee people (also called the Gullah), who are descendants of freed and escaped previously enslaved African Americans who eventually settled in the area, bringing with them a cultural perspective that was passed down through generations. In the Southern US, "haint tales" are deeply rooted in tradition and are an essential aspect of the area's oral and literary traditions. Come with me on an excursion to explore the space between the living and the dead, the ancestral and phantasmal, and the reality-bending sights that haunt those that call these hills their home.

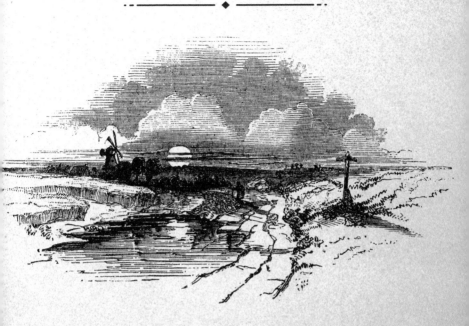

THE MOON-EYED PEOPLE

The Moon-Eyed People is a term used in Southern Appalachian folklore to describe a mysterious group of people who were said to have inhabited certain Southern regions since time immemorial until the Cherokee finally and successfully expelled them. The Moon-Eyed People are said to have had light skin, white beards, and pale, almost translucent, blue, or gray eyes. Their distinctive eye color is believed to be the source of their name. They were subterranean dwellers who lived underground in caves or tunnels, so they were sensitive to sunlight and could only emerge at night, under the light of the moon, also a contributing factor to their name. Whether or not they were actually a product of Native American oral tradition is debatable, but most can acquiesce that these mysterious little men likely did exist and even attribute some of the structural ruins in remote areas deep in the woods to these creatures.

The Moon-Eyed People legend is primarily associated with regions in the southeastern United States, particularly the Appalachian Mountains and parts of North Carolina, Georgia, and Tennessee. Despite the widespread nature of the legend, there is no concrete archaeological or historical evidence to support the existence of the Moon-Eyed People, but the legend lives on as a triumph of the Cherokee who freed settlers from these creepy creatures.

Scholars and historians have various theories about the origins of the Moon-Eyed People legend. Some suggest that the legend may be an attempt to explain interactions with different groups of Indigenous peoples, while others see it as a way to describe ancient migrations or cultural changes over time. It's not that big of a stretch to think there might be a modicum of truth to these ancient stories and even imagine that many such stories of white creatures with beards invading land were at one time prevalent.

AXE HOLLOW MURDERS

Ghost stories, folklore, and legends often blend seamlessly, making it impossible to tell where one ends and the other begins. This is the story of the Axe Hollow murders and the haunting this tragedy spawned. Over the years this story has changed, as young men saw it as a way to frighten their girlfriends. But going back in time, one can trace out the bare framework of the original tale.

At one time, there was a small farm on the road now known as Axe Hollow. The farmer who worked the ground there was a dour man who never seemed to find any happiness in life. His was a dark world, where no one laughed or had joy. It was hard for those who loved him. His wife had become a shadow of a person. There was no romance or love in her life. Hers was a world of work and keeping her husband from being angry. The children, too, suffered because of their father's dark way of looking at the world. They went to school, came home, worked, and were allowed little time to play and enjoy the boundless world around them.

Everything changed one summer when the man hired a drifter as help for the summer farming season. The fellow slept in the barn but always had a smile on his face and a song in his heart. He was quiet but went around humming to himself because he knew his singing annoyed the farmer. It was as if anything with a spark of joy and light had to be extinguished by the sour man.

But for the hired hand, cheerfulness just seemed to come naturally, and he secretly brightened up the world for the little family. He'd send the children in with a beautiful flowers that he found while working in a field. He'd make little toys to please the children and hurried to do a few of their chores before they got home so that they had time to play. All of this was done behind the farmer's back. The man would fret and scream and punish the family if they let him know they found joy in something the hired man did. The farmer probably would have fired the man if he could have, but the fellow worked cheaply and did good work. He simply could not justify firing him.

Perhaps the poor housewife was charmed into infidelity, or perhaps nothing more than kindness transpired between the hired hand and the woman, but the farmer began to suspect that his wife was having an affair with the man. The farmer watched and brooded until he finally drove the man off. That same day, he confronted his wife. His anger was immense, and in his fury, he picked up an axe and swung it at her. He hacked her to death, but still, his rage was not abated. He turned the axe on his children and destroyed them too.

The story states that he was found in the hollow where the road dips down between two large hills, still carrying the axe and muttering to himself. Some people thought he was looking for the hired man while others believed that he was trying to flee the grisly scene he had created in his home. Perhaps he didn't even know where he was or what he had done. In any case, he surrendered easily enough, and he saved the county the trouble of a trial by ending his life on his first night in jail.

That seems to be the original story that circulated long ago. Since then, the story has evolved into an urban legend. It is said that if a young couple parks along the lonely road, the farmer will appear outside the windows of the car swinging his bloody axe. Other versions say that the farmer makes a noise so that the young man in the car will get out, and then he kills them both.

THE APPALACHIAN GRAY MAN

The Appalachian Gray Man is a mysterious and elusive figure associated with paranormal occurrences in the Appalachian Mountains. While similar in name to the Gray Man of Pawleys Island, South Carolina, the Appalachian version has distinct characteristics and lore. Here's what is known about the Appalachian Gray Man:

- The Appalachian Gray Man is often described as a shadowy figure dressed in gray or dark clothing. Witnesses report that he appears on or near mountain trails, usually during adverse weather conditions or moments of danger.

- Like the Gray Man of Pawleys Island, the Appalachian Gray Man is believed to be an omen of danger. Sightings of this figure are said to precede natural disasters, accidents, or other perilous events. Encountering the Gray Man is seen as a forewarning to take precautions or alter one's course. Some versions of the Appalachian Gray Man legend suggest that he acts as a protector of hikers and outdoor enthusiasts. In these accounts, individuals who heed the warning provided by the Gray Man are guided away from potential harm or dangerous situations in the wilderness.

- The Gray Man is sometimes considered a symbol of respect for nature and the Appalachian environment, causing one to speculate on the Indigenous influences on this lore. Encounters with the Gray Man may serve as a reminder to approach the mountains with caution, acknowledging the power and unpredictability of the natural world.

- The story of the Appalachian Gray Man is deeply rooted in the region and passed down through generations. Stories of this mysterious figure often circulate within local communities and align with the cautious warnings and a lesson about respecting the land's resources—a very common theme in many Appalachian stories.

As with many folkloric figures, there are variations in the stories and accounts of sightings. Different communities and individuals may have unique interpretations of the legend, adding to the complexity of the folklore surrounding this mysterious entity. Some interpretations of the Appalachian Gray Man suggest a spiritual or supernatural element to his nature. Whether seen as a ghostly haint or a guardian spirit, the Gray Man embodies the spiritual connection between people and the mountainous landscape, reflecting the relationship between the mountainous terrain, the communities that inhabit it, and the awe-inspiring forces of nature that shape life in the Appalachians.

THE BELL WITCH

The Bell Witch is one of the most famous and enduring ghost stories in Southern Appalachian folklore. It centers around the Bell family, who lived in Adams, Tennessee, in the early nineteenth century. The story is set in the early 1800s, primarily between 1817 and 1821.

The Bell family consisted of John Bell, his wife Lucy, and their children, Betsy and John Jr. The haunting began with strange noises—knocking, tapping, and scratching—heard throughout their farmhouse. Soon, the entity responsible for these disturbances identified itself as "Kate Batts," a ghostly presence believed to be the spirit of a deceased neighbor. Over time, Kate Batts came to be known as the Bell Witch.

The Bell Witch's activities escalated from mere noises to physical attacks on the family members. They reported being slapped, pinched, and even scratched by an invisible force. The entity also had a knack for mimicking voices, often engaging in conversations with the family members and other witnesses. The haunting of the Bell family became widely known, attracting curious neighbors and even some prominent figures from the region. Word of the Bell Witch spread beyond Tennessee, leading to newspaper articles and even a book by Martin Van Buren Ingram, titled *An Authenticated History of the Famous Bell Witch* (WP, 2009).

The witchy entity's motives were unclear. It seemed to have a particular dislike for John Bell Sr., who eventually fell seriously ill and passed away in 1820. The Bell Witch claimed responsibility for his death, declaring that it had poisoned him. After his death, the paranormal activity continued for some time.

The haunting eventually subsided, but it left a lasting legacy in Appalachian and American folklore as a whole. The Bell Witch remains one of the most well-documented and enduring ghost stories in the United States. Numerous books, documentaries, and adaptations have explored the legend, and the Bell Witch Cave in Adams, Tennessee, is a popular tourist attraction associated with the story.

Some theories suggest that the Bell Witch may have been a manifestation of repressed emotions, stress, or was even a hoax. Regardless of its origins, the Bell Witch story holds a significant place in Appalachian folklore and culture.

THE BROWN MOUNTAIN BANSHEES

In the heart of the Blue Ridge Mountains, specifically around Brown Mountain in North Carolina, an eerie phenomenon has captured the imaginations of locals for generations—the Brown Mountain Lights. These spectral lights, said to dance and flicker mysteriously over the mountain, are often accompanied by tales of a ghostly presence known as the Brown Mountain Banshees.

Legend has it that, on certain nights, when the air is thick with otherworldly energy, the Brown Mountain Banshees make their presence known. These supernatural entities are said to be ethereal and elusive, floating alongside the mysterious lights that illuminate the mountain. Witnesses claim that the banshees emit ghostly wails, their piercing cries echoing through the valleys and adding an extra layer of strangeness to the already mysterious lights.

Local folklore suggests that the Brown Mountain Banshees are the spirits of Native American maidens, heartbroken and restless due to tragic love stories that unfolded in the ancient past, although it's unlikely this was ever part of true Native American oral tradition. But as the lights appear and the penetrative cries echo off the mountainsides, it is easy to imagine that the banshees are searching for their lost loves or, perhaps, resisting their untimely fates. Some stories paint a vivid picture of the banshees as ethereal figures with flowing hair, clad in garments reminiscent of a bygone era. Their cries are said to carry both sorrow and a warning, acting as a spectral beacon for those who witness the mysterious lights.

THE PHANTOM FUNERAL PROCESSION OF CUMBERLAND GAP

A ghostly tale unfolds in the hills and valleys surrounding Cumberland Gap—a story known as the Phantom Funeral Procession. Legends speak of an otherworldly event that transpires in the dead of night, where the ethereal echoes of a long-lost funeral procession make their haunting presence known.

According to the lore passed from generation to generation, the Phantom Funeral Procession is said to materialize along a desolate stretch of road near Cumberland Gap in Virginia, a significant roadway and mountain pass steeped in history and mystery. The phantom procession is said to manifest under the veil of darkness, taking the form of a solemn procession of mourners clad in attire reminiscent of a bygone era.

Witnesses who have dared to venture along the haunted path describe a spectral cortege led by an unseen hearse, followed by mourners in old-fashioned funeral attire. The sound of ghostly hoofbeats and rattling carriage wheels accompanies the procession, creating an eerie symphony that reverberates through the night. The mourners are believed to be ghosts caught in a perpetual state of grief, reenacting a funeral ceremony that took place in the distant past.

Local legends offer different interpretations of the origins of this haunting phenomenon. Some attribute it to the restless spirits of soldiers who perished in the tumultuous battles of the region during the Civil War era, while others connect it to the tragic tale of a funeral procession gone awry, forever imprinted on the spiritual fabric of Cumberland Gap.

THE HAUNTING OF THE GROVER PARK INN

The Grover Park Inn, located in Asheville, North Carolina, is steeped in ghostly tales and mysterious happenings. Built in 1913, this historic hotel has a complicated history that weighs heavily with stories of paranormal activity.

One of the most famous ghostly residents in all of Appalachia is the Pink Lady. Legend has it that a young woman fell to her death from a balcony during the 1920s. Some guests claim to have encountered her spirit, describing a pink mist or the scent of lavender in their rooms.

There are also reports of strange occurrences, specifically in Room 545, where the spirit of a young child named Laura supposedly resides. Guests have mentioned hearing laughter and the sound of bouncing balls, even when the room is unoccupied.

The Inn's employees have shared their own eerie experiences, including sightings of shadowy figures and unexplained noises. The historic setting and the hotel's long history contribute to the mystique that surrounds The Grover Park Inn, making it a destination not only for those seeking comfort but also for those intrigued by the possibility of encountering the supernatural. You may not get a peaceful night's rest, but you will definitely have a story to tell.

THE GHOSTS OF CUMBERLAND FALLS

Cumberland Falls, nestled in the Daniel Boone National Forest of Kentucky, is not only renowned for its stunning beauty and supreme vistas but also for the phantasmal legends surrounding it.

One of the most famous stories involves a spectral figure known as the Moonbow Ghost. As the legend goes, a man fell to his death while trying to retrieve his wife's scarf that had blown into the falls. It is said that on clear nights when the moonbow (a nighttime rainbow caused by the light of the moon) graces the waterfall, the ghostly figure of the man can be seen searching for his lost love.

Another tale revolves around the tragic fate of a Native American woman and her lover. Forbidden to be together, they leaped from the cliffs near the falls, choosing death over separation. Visitors claim to hear the woman's mournful cries echoing in the night.

These ghost stories, intertwined with the natural beauty of Cumberland Falls, add an eerie and mystical aura to this enchanting destination, inviting travelers to experience both the wonders of nature and the haunting mysteries that linger in the moonlit shadows.

THE SPIRITS OF THE OVERMOUNTAIN MEN

In the heart of the Southern Appalachian Mountains, a brave group of patriots known as the Overmountain Men stood ready to defend their homeland from British tyranny. These fearless souls hailed from the rugged frontier, and they were as tough as the towering peaks that surrounded them.

As the winds of revolution swept across the land, the Overmountain Men heard the call to arms. They knew that the fate of their fledgling nation hung in the balance, and they were determined to do their part.

The most famous chapter in their story unfolded in the autumn of 1780, when they received word of a British invasion. The infamous British Major Patrick Ferguson was leading a force towards them, determined to crush the rebellion. The Overmountain Men gathered their rifles, donned their hunting shirts, and embarked on an epic journey to meet the enemy head-on.

Their path led them through dense forests, treacherous mountain passes, and rushing rivers. They faced hunger, exhaustion, and the ever-present threat of attack. But their spirits remained unbroken as they pressed on towards destiny.

Finally, on a crisp October morning, they reached the fateful battleground known as Kings Mountain. There, amid the swirling smoke and deafening musket fire, the Overmountain Men fought with a ferocity born of their unyielding love for liberty.

In the end, they emerged victorious, having turned the tide of the Revolutionary War in favor of the American cause.

Major Ferguson lay dead, and his forces were scattered. The spirit of the Overmountain Men had prevailed.

But the story doesn't end on that historic battlefield. As the years rolled by, and the nation they helped forge grew, the spirits of those brave men were said to linger in the mountains they loved so dearly.

Many travelers and hikers in the Southern Appalachians have reported strange encounters on moonlit nights. They've glimpsed shadowy figures in old-fashioned attire, the very image of those Overmountain Men. Some say they've heard the distant echoes of musket fire and the faint cadence of long-forgotten battle cries.

These encounters are a testament to the enduring spirit of those fearless patriots. They remind us that the legacy of the Overmountain Men lives on, not only in the history books but also in the very land itself.

So, next time you find yourself in the heart of the Southern Appalachians, keep an eye out for the spirits of the Overmountain Men.

THE GHOST LIGHTS OF THOMAS DIVIDE

The haunting phenomenon of the Thomas Divide Lights has captured the imaginations of both locals and visitors to the Great Smoky Mountains of North Carolina for generations. These mysterious illuminations, which appear sporadically along the mountain pass, have inspired several legends, each rich with cultural significance and historical resonance. Among these tales, one particularly poignant story centers around a Cherokee shaman, whom not only speaks to the supernatural, but also echoes the tragic history of the Cherokee people in this region.

According to this version of the legend, during the era of the Trail of Tears in the 1830s—a time of forced removal and immense suffering for the Cherokee—a shaman of profound wisdom and respect decided to resist the U.S. government's edicts. He believed that his spiritual connection and ancestral duties to the land could not be severed, prompting him and his family to seek refuge deep within the familiar yet foreboding mountains, which they had long called home.

The story unfolds with the shaman using ancient knowledge and the cover of the dense mountain forests to evade capture. However, the relentless soldiers eventually tracked down the shaman and his family. In a brutal display meant to deter other Cherokee from attempting to stay behind, the shaman was captured, executed, and horrifically dismembered. His remains were scattered across the vastness of the mountains as a chilling warning to others.

It is said that the eerie lights seen weaving through the trees and over the misty peaks of Thomas Divide are manifestations of the shaman's restless spirit. These lights represent his ongoing search across the mountainous terrain to reunite the scattered parts of his body so that he might finally rest in peace. The lights are described as silent, solemn, and persistent, reflecting the determination of a spirit wronged by history, yet undeterred in its quest for wholeness and dignity.

The legend intertwines with other folkloric interpretations of the lights, including tales of the Cherokee Little People—mystical beings believed to protect the tribe and its secrets—whose lanterns light up the night as they move through the forest. Another interpretation involves Judaculla, a mythical giant in Cherokee lore, known for his supernatural powers and whose fireballs, thrown in anger or protection, light up the night sky.

These stories are deeply rooted in the cultural memory of the Cherokee and the broader Appalachian folklore. They serve not only as entertainment but as a form of oral history that preserves and honors the heritage of the Cherokee people. The legends highlight their deep spiritual connection to the land, their resilience in the face of adversity, and their enduring presence in the mountains.

The Thomas Divide Overlook, from which many have claimed to see these spectral illuminations, bears the name of William Thomas, a significant figure in Cherokee history. As a white chief of the Cherokee during the 1830s and 1840s, Thomas played a crucial role in establishing the Qualla Boundary, which allowed some members of the Cherokee to remain in their ancestral mountains. This area, preserved amidst the forced relocations, became a sanctuary of cultural preservation and is a testament to the enduring spirit of the Cherokee people.

Today, the story of the Thomas Divide Lights, particularly the legend of the Cherokee shaman, is a poignant reminder of the past. It invites reflection on the injustices endured by the Native Americans and the spiritual depth that characterizes much of Native American folklore.

THE CURSED VILLAGE OF DAMASCUS

Situated amid the rolling hills and ancient forests of the Southern Appalachians, the village of Damascus seemed, at first glance, like any other. Its charming cottages and friendly residents created an idyllic picture of rural life. But beneath this picturesque façade lurked a darkness that would chill the hearts of anyone who delved into its history.

It was said that the curse descended upon Damascus many generations ago, in a time when the village was home to a close-knit community of settlers. They lived harmoniously with the land, working the fields, and tending to their livestock, until one fateful day when a wandering traveler came to town.

The stranger was an obscure figure, with a hooded cloak that concealed their features. They spoke in hushed whispers of ancient rituals and arcane powers, offering the villagers a tantalizing promise—wealth beyond imagination and power beyond reckoning.

Driven by greed and curiosity, the villagers gathered in secret to perform the traveler's dark rituals. They danced beneath the moonlight, their chants echoing through the night as they summoned forces they could not comprehend.

But as the rituals reached their climax, a terrible realization struck the villagers—the traveler was not what they seemed. With a wicked laugh, the hooded figure revealed themselves to be a malevolent being, a creature of darkness and despair.

The ground trembled, and the skies roared with thunder as the curse descended upon Damascus. The very land rebelled, swallowing homes, crops, and lives into an abyss of eternal

darkness. The once-thriving village was reduced to ruins, its legacy forever tainted by the folly of its residents.

In the years that followed, the cursed village of Damascus became a place of dread and despair. Those who dared to approach its crumbling remnants spoke of restless haints, tortured souls doomed to wander the land in eternal torment. Shadows danced along the moonlit streets, and unsettling wails pierced the night.

Legend has it that the curse still lingers, waiting to ensnare the unwary and to exact its vengeance upon those who dare to trespass upon the forsaken village. Travelers who venture too close speak of a sense of foreboding, as if an unseen presence watches their every move.

THE HIKER'S GHOST TRAIN

The tale of the Hiker's Ghost Train begins on a misty, moonlit night. A group of adventurous hikers, drawn by the lure of the Appalachian wilderness, embarked on a journey to traverse the old, abandoned tracks. They sought to challenge themselves, to conquer the very path that had once been so vital to the region.

The hikers began their expedition with excitement, carrying backpacks filled with supplies and lanterns to light their way. They followed the disused tracks, their footsteps echoing through the silent woods as they ventured deeper into the wilderness.

As they walked, the hikers shared stories and laughter, unaware of the history that clung to the very ground beneath them. For you see, it was on these very tracks that a tragic incident had occurred decades ago—a horrific train derailment that claimed the lives of many.

As the hikers continued their journey, an eerie sensation overcame them. The air grew colder, and the forest fell into an oppressive silence. It was then that they heard it—a distant, solitary whistle, the sound of a train in the dead of night.

Panic seized the group as they shone their lanterns down the tracks, desperately searching for the source of the chilling noise. And then, emerging from the ethereal mist, a spectral train materialized before their very eyes—an ancient locomotive, adorned with tattered banners and bathed in an eerie, ethereal light.

The hikers watched in awe and terror as the ghostly train roared past them, the ground trembling beneath its phantom

wheels. The specter was unlike any train they had ever seen—its cars filled with long-dead passengers, their eyes hollow and empty, and their faces etched with sorrow.

The hikers could only watch as the Hiker's Ghost Train disappeared into the night, its haunted whistle fading into the distance. They were left in stunned silence, shaken to their very core by the otherworldly encounter.

Some say that the Hiker's Ghost Train is a manifestation of the souls lost in the tragic derailment—restless haints forever condemned to roam the Appalachian wilderness. Others believe it serves as a warning, a reminder of the perils that lurk within the ancient forests.

THE PHANTOM FIRE WATCHER OF ROARING FORK

Roaring Fork Motor Nature Trail can be found in the lush embrace of the Smoky Mountains. By day, it's a serene and picturesque drive, with winding roads that meander through towering trees and babbling brooks. But when night falls and the woods are shrouded in darkness, this tranquil trail transforms into a realm of mystery and the supernatural.

The story begins many decades ago, during a time when the Great Smoky Mountains were plagued by wildfires that raged through the thickets and underbrush. In response to this peril, a brave and dedicated fire watcher named Samuel took on the solemn duty of protecting the forest from the devastating infernos.

Samuel was known throughout the region as a man of unwavering resolve, a solitary figure who'd spend his nights perched high in the fire tower at Roaring Fork, watching vigilantly for signs of trouble. His humble cabin stood nearby, a place where he'd rest during the day before ascending the tower once more when night fell.

One fateful evening, as darkness enshrouded the forest, Samuel climbed the tower to begin his nightly watch. He scanned the landscape, his trained eyes seeking out any flicker of flame or telltale wisp of smoke.

Hours passed, and Samuel's diligence never waned. He remained steadfast, his only companions the howling wind and the chorus of nocturnal creatures that serenaded the night.

But then, as the witching hour approached, Samuel witnessed something that would forever haunt his memory. Through the

thick canopy of trees, he spotted an eerie, ghostly light
flickering in the distance. It danced and swayed, defying
explanation, and its macabre glow sent a chill down his spine.

Samuel knew the dangers of the forest better than anyone,
and he couldn't ignore this unnatural phenomenon. Leaving his
post in the fire tower, he descended into the darkness, lantern
in hand, to investigate the source of the mysterious light.

As he ventured deeper into the woods, the light seemed
to beckon him onward, leading him through tangled
underbrush and winding trails. The trees themselves seemed
to whisper secrets, and the night air grew heavy with an
inexplicable energy.

And then, as Samuel rounded a bend in the trail, he came face to face with the haint—a spectral figure bathed in an ethereal, pale blue light. It was a woman, her form translucent and her eyes filled with sadness. She was dressed in clothing that seemed out of place, from a bygone era.

The woman extended her hand toward Samuel, her voice barely a whisper, as she implored him for help. She spoke of a fire that had consumed her family's cabin long ago, a fire that had claimed their lives and left her spirit bound to the forest.

Unable to resist her plea, Samuel followed the ghostly woman deeper into the woods. She led him to the remnants of a long-forgotten cabin, its charred timbers standing as a testament to the tragedy that had unfolded there.

With each step, the ghostly woman's form grew fainter, her figure dissipating like morning mist. But before she vanished completely, she turned to Samuel and uttered a haunting thank you, her voice fading into the night.

From that night onward, Samuel became a changed man. He could never explain the supernatural encounter he'd experienced, nor could he ignore the bond he'd formed with the phantom fire-watcher of Roaring Fork.

Some say that Samuel continued to watch over the forest, not only for the threat of wildfires but also as a guardian for the restless spirits that lingered within. To this day, hikers and visitors to the Great Smoky Mountains speak of strange lights and dreadful whispers that haunt the Roaring Fork Motor Nature Trail, a reminder of Samuel's encounter with the supernatural—a reminder, too, that, in the depths of the ancient forest, mysteries and spirits await those who dare to seek them out.

THE HAUNTED SHELTERS

Beneath the beauty of the Appalachian Trail lies a series of mysterious and spine-tingling legends. These stories have been passed down through generations of hikers and locals, and they speak of supernatural occurrences that defy explanation.

Our tale begins with a shelter known as the Roan High Knob Shelter. Perched high in the Roan Highlands, it offers breathtaking vistas of the surrounding mountains. By day, it's a haven for weary hikers, a place to rest and take in the majesty of the Appalachian landscape. But as night falls, the atmosphere changes.

Hikers who have stayed at the Roan High Knob Shelter report strange noises in the night—whispers carried on the wind, ghostly footsteps echoing through the woods, and the chilling sensation of being watched by unseen eyes. Legend has it that the shelter is haunted by the spirits of long-departed hikers who met untimely ends on the trail.

Farther south along the trail, nestled deep in the Smoky Mountains, lies the Spence Field Shelter. This shelter, surrounded by lush meadows and wildflowers, seems idyllic by day. But at night, it becomes the stage for an freaky phenomenon.

Hikers who have stayed at the Spence Field Shelter speak of ghostly lights that dance among the trees, illuminating the night with an abnormal glow. Some believe these lights are the spirits of Cherokee warriors who once roamed these lands, while others think they are the restless souls of hikers who perished on the trail.

Then there's the infamous Davis Path Shelter. This shelter, located in New Hampshire's White Mountains, has earned a sinister reputation. Hikers who spend the night there often report feelings of unease, as if an unseen presence is lurking in the shadows.

Some claim to have heard disembodied voices in the dead of night, whispering words that send shivers down their spines. Others have seen ghostly figures, their forms flickering like candle flames in the darkness.

As we venture deeper into the heart of the Appalachian wilderness, we encounter the Watauga Lake Shelter in Tennessee. This remote shelter is surrounded by dense forest and overlooks a tranquil lake. But peace is not always the prevailing sensation.

Hikers who have camped here have shared stories of a spectral figure that roams the area, a figure known as the Watauga Lake Woman. She is said to be the spirit of a young woman who met a tragic end near the shelter many years ago. She is often seen weeping by the water's edge, her sorrowful cries echoing through the night.

THE LADY IN WHITE OF THE SHENANDOAH VALLEY

In the quiet, rolling hills of Virginia's Shenandoah Valley, where the Blue Ridge Mountains stand as sentinels, there lies a tale that has been whispered among the locals for generations. It's a story that begins on a moonlit night, much like the one we find ourselves under tonight.

Our tale unfolds in the 1800s, a time when the Shenandoah Valley was still a wilderness, and the towns were small and close-knit. Among these towns was a picturesque village nestled by the banks of the Shenandoah River. Life was simple, and the community thrived on hard work and unity.

In this village lived a young woman named Eleanor, a name that would become synonymous with the legend of the Lady in White. Eleanor was known far and wide for her beauty; her ebony hair framed her pale face and her eyes were as blue as the clear skies that stretched over the valley.

But Eleanor was more than just a pretty face. She was kindhearted, generous, and beloved by all who knew her. It was said that she had a special connection to the natural world, a gift for healing and understanding the secrets of the forest.

One fateful evening, as the sun dipped below the horizon and cast long shadows over the valley, Eleanor set out to visit her lover, a young man from a neighboring town named Samuel. They had promised to meet by the river's edge, beneath the ancient oak tree that stood as a sentinel to their love.

But as Eleanor made her way through the darkening woods, her heart sank with each passing moment. Samuel was nowhere to be found. Hours felt like eternity, and still, there was no sign of her beloved.

Desperate and afraid, Eleanor clung to the hope that Samuel had been delayed, that he would arrive soon with a heartfelt apology and a promise never to be late again. But as the night wore on, her hope turned to dread.

As the first light of dawn crept over the mountains, Eleanor's search came to a devastating end. She found Samuel's lifeless body, his eyes forever closed, his love forever lost. It was a tragedy that would haunt the valley for generations to come.

Eleanor's grief was all-consuming. She could not bear the thought of a life without Samuel, and so, in her despair, she made a choice that would bind her to the valley for all eternity. She donned a flowing white gown, the color of mourning, and wandered into the wilderness.

From that day forward, the villagers spoke of a ghostly figure—a lady in white—wandering the valley, her searching cries echoing through the night. They say that she searches for her lost love, that she is forever bound to the Shenandoah Valley, unable to find peace until she is reunited with Samuel.

Over the years, countless souls have claimed to have seen the Lady in White. She is said to appear on moonlit nights, her ethereal form drifting through the trees, her wraithlike cries piercing the stillness. Some say she reaches out to passersby, as if seeking comfort or guidance, while others claim she vanishes into thin air when approached.

THE LOST COLONY OF ROANOKE

The Lost Colony of Roanoke is a captivating mystery that has puzzled historians and intrigued storytellers for centuries. In the late sixteenth century, Sir Walter Raleigh, an English explorer, sponsored the establishment of the Roanoke Colony on the coast of what is now North Carolina.

In 1587, John White led a group of colonists, which included men, women, and children, to settle in Roanoke. However, due to various challenges, including scarce resources and strained relations with the local Native American tribes, White returned to England for supplies, leaving behind his daughter, son-in-law, and granddaughter, Virginia Dare—the first English child born in the New World.

When White returned to Roanoke in 1590, he discovered a mystery that endures to this day—the colony had vanished without a trace. The only clue was the word "CROATOAN" carved into a post and "CRO" carved into a nearby tree. These mysterious markings fueled speculation and sparked the enduring legend of the Lost Colony.

Numerous theories attempt to explain the disappearance, ranging from assimilation into Native American communities, to harsh weather conditions or conflict with neighboring tribes. The lack of concrete evidence has allowed the Lost Colony of Roanoke to become one of America's greatest historical mysteries, leaving historians and storytellers alike to weave their interpretations into the rich tapestry of the nation's past.

CRYPTIDS AND HYBRIDS

In the mysterious shadows of the Appalachian wilderness, where the ancient forests whisper secrets and the rivers hum their age-old songs, lies a world teeming with creatures that defy the boundaries of imagination. Here, amid the dense undergrowth and shadowy hollows, lurk beings both fearsome and fantastical, born from the depths of human imagination and the wild whispers of the land itself. From the elusive creatures that haunt the remote peaks to the peculiar hybrids that roam the moonlit valleys, each legend holds a kernel of truth, waiting to be unearthed by those brave enough to venture into the unknown. From the legendary Mothman that swoops the skies to the enigmatic Wampus Cat that prowls the forests, prepare to delve into a world where the extraordinary becomes ordinary and the mundane fades into obscurity. As we delve deeper into the mysteries of the Appalachian wilderness, we will uncover tales of strange encounters, eerie sightings, and whispered legends passed down through generations.

CRYPTIDS

Cryptids are creepy animals that live hidden in the forests and terrain of much of the world, but in America, particularly in Appalachia, they seem to be most common. Cryptozoologists maintain that cryptids are likely real creatures, but, as is typical with otherworldly-seeming creatures, there is no substantiated scientific proof of their existence. However, aside from direct eye-witnesses, one might discover large footprints that could only belong to a massive bipedal creature, or slime clinging to a tree that can only have come from something creepy, unexplained, and most certainly alive. You have likely heard of—or even personally seen—one of America's most legendary cryptids, Bigfoot, or maybe you've spotted a lizard-looking man dashing between the trees in the Scape Ore Swamp. If that's the case, then you are one of the lucky few who have witnessed these lurking beasts. . .if *lucky* is the right word.

WAMPUS CAT

Deep in the Northern Appalachian Mountains, there exists a creature that has long captured the imagination of its inhabitants. The Wampus Cat, also known as the Cherokee Death Cat, is a prominent figure in regional folklore.

Imagine, if you will, a creature that defies convention, a beast described as a petrifying fusion between a mountain lion and a woman. To those who ardently believe in its existence, the Wampus Cat prowls the Appalachian wilderness, its mere presence accompanied by eerie and spine-chilling sounds that reverberate through the woods, sending shivers down the spines of those unfortunate enough to cross its path.

Cherokee folklore, with its rich tapestry of stories, offers an intriguing glimpse into the enigma of the Wampus Cat and the people themselves. Among the numerous legends lies the story of Running Deer, a Cherokee woman whose heart burned with a desire for vengeance against the malevolent spirit known as Ew'ah, the Spirit of Madness. Running Deer believed that this spirit had driven her husband, Standing Bear, to the brink of madness.

Armed with a traditional Cherokee "booger mask" used in the Appalachian region's ceremonial Booger Dance, and embodying the spirit of a mountain cat, Running Deer embarked on a quest to defeat Ew'ah. The encounter resulted in a violent fight that Running Deer ultimately won. Her triumph transformed her into the tribe's revered Spirit-Talker and Home-Protector, taking the shape of the woman she was in combination with the enemy she defeated. Some suggest that the spirit of Running Deer endures within the Wampus Cat of today, a vigilant guardian of Cherokee lands against the hidden forces lurking within the depths of Tanasi.

In another iteration of the tale, the Wampus Cat emerges from the punishment of a woman who dared to trespass upon a sacred ceremony by concealing herself beneath the pelt of a mountain lion. A stern medicine man's retribution took the form of the terrifying feline entity, forever binding her to the Appalachian landscape as the Wampus Cat.

Throughout the vast expanse of the region surrounding Connecticut, the Wampus Cat dons many monikers, from the elusive Gallywampus to the evocative Whistling Wampus. Its appearances are rumored to be most frequent at twilight or dawn, casting eerie shadows upon the Appalachian landscape and omitting an almost human-sounding cry, oft mistaken for a woman's wail. Within the fire-side whispers of Appalachian folklore, this mythical entity often assumes the form of a feline manifestation of a cursed woman, bearing the weight of her disobedience or purported dealings with witchcraft.

Some interpretations suggest the markers of European mythologies, particularly the lore of shape-shifting witches and women possessing the dark hearts of the wicked. These old-world colonial influences seamlessly merged with the distinctive folkloric tales of the Cherokee.

Eyewitness accounts paint a vivid portrait of the Wampus Cat. It is depicted as a hulking and menacing creature, sporting a face reminiscent of a bobcat. This mysterious entity straddles the boundary between feline and human, boasting a visage adorned with sharp, elongated claws and fearsome fangs. Yet, its most haunting feature is its eyes—piercing, luminescent yellow orbs that seemingly slice through the darkest recesses of the Appalachian night.

Reports by terrified victims further embellish this cryptid's physicality. Its sinewy, muscular form is shrouded in coarse, matted fur, and it is often accompanied by a long, serpentine tail—perfect for maintaining balance and dexterity. Some narratives even suggest that the creature boasts six legs, leading to intriguing conjectures of a spiderlike cat that makes its way across the terrain with each spindly leg working independently of each other in a gruesome display of cryptic mobility and agility.

Sightings of the Wampus Cat have been sporadic, typically unfolding in the depths of dense, unforgiving forests or remote, untamed landscapes. Those who have ventured upon this mysterious entity describe an overwhelming sensation of unease—an acute awareness of being under its penetrating gaze that is felt before confirmed.

The Wampus Cat is believed to harbor supernatural capabilities, with one of its most prominent attributes being its bone-chilling vocalizations. These eerie cries, a spookish blend of feline growls and fearful humanoid utterances, are thought to serve as a means of attracting prey, warding off potential threats, or warning the vulnerable of tragedy and demise.

The creature is further attributed with astonishing speed and stealth, affording it the ability to navigate the densest Appalachian woodlands and elude detection with ease. Legends posit that it possesses the uncanny power to shape-shift or become invisible, elevating its cryptic status to even greater heights.

THE WOLF MAN OF KENTUCKY

The story of the Wolf Man of Kentucky begins in the remote and untamed reaches of the southern Appalachian wilderness, where civilization yields to the primeval and the boundary between the notorious and the obscure becomes blurred. Cryptids, those elusive and mysterious creatures that dwell at the edge of human understanding, often find their home in such wild and uncharted territories.

This legend centers around a creature that defies conventional categorization—a perplexing blend of man and wolf. While tales of wolf-men and werewolves can be traced across time and cultures, the existence of a wolf-human hybrid of the Kentucky variety is traced back to the early nineteenth century when pioneers and settlers in the Kentucky Hills first began sharing chilling tales of a feral and beastly being that roamed the night, gnashing its ferocious teeth and omitting a solitary cry that rippled the waters of the streams and wilted the mountain grasses.

Described as a monstrous amalgamation of human and lupine features, the Wolf Man of Kentucky is said to stand on two legs, much like a regular man, yet possesses the physical attributes of a wolf. Witnesses who claim to have encountered this cryptid describe it as having a human face framed by fur-covered ears and crowned with a tangled mane of unkempt hair . . . or fur: no living soul has come close enough to check and make sure.

Its body is often described as a grotesque fusion of human and wolf, with long, sinewy limbs ending in powerful, clawed, humanoid hands and feet. His eyes, a mesmerizing blend of human intelligence and feral instinct, exude an eerie luminescence that pierces the inky blackness of the Appalachian night.

Eyewitness accounts of the Wolf Man of Kentucky are chilling, to say the least. Those who have crossed paths with this unpredictable (and rather inhospitable) cryptid recount tales of terror that defy explanation. The creature is believed to have an insatiable appetite for the flesh of animals and, some claim, people as well. In the dark cover of night, it prowls through the dense woodlands and foothills, emitting bone-chilling howls that send shivers down the spines of those who hear them. The creature's unearthly vocalizations strike fear into the hearts of anyone who dares to venture into the untamed wilderness, leaving a lasting impression of dread and a strong desire to never go back.

As with many cryptid legends, theories abound regarding the origins and nature of the Wolf Man of Kentucky. Some believe it to be a product of folklore and imagination, a cautionary tale spun around campfires to discourage reckless exploration of the wilderness. Others, however, maintain that there may be a kernel of truth buried within the legend. They suggest that the Wolf Man could be an undiscovered species or a genetic anomaly—a creature that defies the traditional boundaries of the animal kingdom, but one that does, indeed, exist, nevertheless.

THE MOTHMAN OF MASON COUNTY

The Mothman is a mysterious figure hailing from Point Pleasant, West Virginia, that has captured the imagination of many and has become an integral part of urban legends, historical lore, and popular culture. It's often classified as a cryptid due to its elusive nature and some reports of it seeming to be composed of two or more earthly animals, but its exact appearance seems to slightly vary depending on who is recalling an encounter. Some say this is because it can take on the characteristics of your darkest and innermost nightmares, others say it is because it is a reflection of the darkness in one's own soul.

But the name "Mothman" was coined by the press, inspired by the creature's purported appearance as a large humanoid figure with wings that resemble those of a moth. It is said to far outsize a human man, standing at around 7 to 10 feet tall (2 to 3 m) and has large, glowing red eyes that are described as hypnotic or entrancing. Its expansive wings enable it to fly silently and with great speed. Some accounts suggest that the wingspan can reach up to 10 feet (3 m).

The Mothman is primarily known for the series of reported sightings across Mason Couty, between 1966 and 1967. Witnesses claimed to have seen this winged creature swooping in circles, like a vulture awaiting death, over the town and the nearby abandoned TNT area—a site used during World War II for the manufacturing and storage of explosives. It has also famously divebombed cars, running unsuspecting drivers off the road and blinding them in the dark with its brightly glowing eyes. The victims of Mothman encounters describe overwhelming feelings of intense fear, dread, or a sense of impending disaster and death. Some believe that the creature is a portent of doom or a warning of tragic events.

The most famous sighting occurred on December 15, 1967, when the Silver Bridge in Point Pleasant collapsed, resulting in the deaths of forty-six people. Some locals believe the Mothman's presence was somehow connected to the disaster. Various theories have emerged to explain the Mothman phenomenon. Skeptics often attribute the sightings to misidentifications of birds, owls, or other natural creatures, while others consider it a mass hysteria or a result of psychological stress in the community. One thing's for sure, I've never seen a bird like that.

Paranormal investigators suggest that the Mothman is a supernatural entity, possibly an alien, interdimensional being, or a messenger of disaster, sent to warn or predict tragic events. Some cryptozoologists classify the Mothman as a sort of cryptid, a creature that defies conventional knowledge of the beasts who roam this Earth and has not been scientifically documented or verified but who makes appearances in many unrelated contexts. In this case, it has been seen as a potentially unknown species or a creature that defies conventional biological classifications. Is it real? I dare you to go find out.

THE SHEEPSQUATCH

While on a day hike on the Appalachian Trail in West Virginia, a pleasant outdoorsman might whiff the rather unpleasant smell of sulfur. This is a signal to run or they might encounter the dreaded Sheepsquatch, a baffling creature of the cryptid variety, being that it has the head of a sheep (horns and all) but the body and wooly fur of a Sasquatch. It has raccoon-paw-like hands and the hairless tail of an overgrown rat. Sightings of the Sheepsquatch are rare but consistent enough to maintain its status as a local legend. The majority of reported encounters occur in the rural and heavily wooded areas of southern West Virginia. Witnesses often describe feelings of dread and unease when they come across the creature, which is said to emit guttural, unsettling sounds.

One of the most well-known Sheepsquatch sightings occurred in 1994 in Boone County. A group of friends claimed to have encountered the creature while camping in the woods. They reported a terrifying experience involving the Sheepsquatch attacking their campsite, ripping their tents to shreds, and trampling their supplies, the creature leaving only ruins in its wake. While the story was met with skepticism by some, the residents of Boone County had dealt with creatures before, and so many of them believed the harrowing account.

Theories abound on the Sheepsquatch phenomenon. Skeptics argue that these sightings may be attributed to misidentified wildlife, such as bears or large dogs, or even hoaxes designed to perpetuate local legends. Others propose that the Sheepsquatch is a product of folklore, emerging from tales and stories passed down through whispering generations.

THE DWAYYO

The Dwayyo, also known as the Maryland Dogman, is a cryptid creature with a long history of sightings and encounters in the state of Maryland, particularly in the areas around the city of Baltimore. This mysterious creature is often described as a wolflike or doglike creature with some characteristics resembling a humanoid figure.

Witnesses who claim to have encountered the Dwayyo describe it as a large, bipedal creature that stands upright like a human. It's covered in dark or shaggy fur, often described as black or brown, similar to that of a wolf or a large dog. The creature is reported to have sharp teeth and powerful jaws.

The Dwayyo is said to be quite tall, with estimates ranging from 7 to 9 feet (2 to 2.7 m) in height when standing upright.

Witnesses note its muscular build, adding to its overall intimidating appearance.

Reports suggest that the Dwayyo is a nocturnal creature, typically active during the night. It is often associated with aggressive howling or growling sounds, which can be unsettling to those who have heard them. Some accounts also describe it as being highly agile and capable of swift movement.

Sightings of the Dwayyo have occurred sporadically over the years and some witnesses claim to have seen the creature near forests, parks, or even suburban areas. Encounters often leave those who witness the creature in a state of shock or fear due to its unusual and terrifying appearance.

The Dwayyo has become a part of local folklore in Maryland, with numerous stories and legends passed down through generations. Some tales depict the creature as a menacing and malevolent being, while others suggest that it primarily keeps to itself and avoids human contact. As with many cryptid creatures, there is speculation about what the Dwayyo might be. Some theories propose that it could be a misidentified known animal, such as a large dog or wolf, while others entertain the possibility of it being a new or undiscovered species. Skeptics often attribute Dwayyo sightings to hoaxes or imaginative storytelling.

The Dwayyo has captured the imagination of locals, inspiring stories, books, and even artwork. It has become a part of Maryland's cultural identity and adds an element of mystery to the state's folklore.

THE SNALLYGASTER

The Snallygaster is a cryptid creature from American folklore, primarily associated with the Appalachian region, particularly Maryland. This fearsome and mysterious creature has captured the imaginations of locals and cryptozoologists alike. This cryptic creature is often described as a bizarre and terrifying hybrid beast. Commonly reported to have a body resembling a large bird or reptile, it has features such as enormous bat-like wings, sharp talons, a long beak, and rows of teeth. Some accounts even suggest it has octopus-like tentacles.

The name "Snallygaster" is thought to have originated from the German immigrants who settled in the region. It combines the German word *schneller geist*, meaning "quick spirit" or "fast ghost," with the English word "gaster," which means "belly" or "stomach."

The legend of the Snallygaster dates back to the early nineteenth century when it terrorized the residents of Frederick County, Maryland, and neighboring areas. Newspapers from the time reported sightings and encounters with this mysterious creature. Local folklore suggests it was a menace to livestock, often described as a predator that would swoop down to snatch animals away.

According to legend, the Snallygaster possesses a variety of abilities and attributes that add to its frightening reputation. It is said to emit a blood-curdling scream or screech, which could be heard from miles away and would freeze the blood of those who heard it. Some stories also mention its ability to suck the blood of its victims. In Maryland folklore, the Snallygaster is sometimes pitted against another cryptid, Dwayyo, the Maryland Dogman. These two creatures are said to be adversaries, with epic battles occurring in local legends. Even the famous American author Mark Twain claimed to have encountered the Snallygaster during his travels through Maryland. He described it as "half reptile, half bird" and recounted how the local citizens believed in its existence.

The Snallygaster was a source of genuine fear and anxiety for the people of Frederick County in the nineteenth century. Many locals were genuinely terrified of the creature, and some even took measures to protect themselves from potential attacks. Hex signs in the shape of a star are painted on barns to warn the beast away. While some might argue that these are just beautiful works of art, many locals still see these as ways to protect against supernatural forces.

Over time, the Snallygaster legend has been associated with hoaxes and practical jokes. In the early twentieth century, a series of sensationalized newspaper articles and reports about the Snallygaster were revealed to be hoaxes. Despite this, the creature continues to be a part of local culture and has appeared in various forms in pop culture, including books, movies, and even craft beer labels.

In recent years, the Snallygaster has evolved from a feared creature into a mascot of sorts for Frederick County, Maryland. The town hosts an annual "Snallygaster Beer Festival" where craft beer enthusiasts gather to celebrate the creature and sample unique brews.

THE TENNESSEE WILD MAN

The Tennessee Wild Man, also known as the "Wildman of Nolichucky," is a legendary cryptid-type creature reported to inhabit the wild and remote areas of Tennessee, particularly in the Nolichucky River Valley. The creature is described as a large, hairy, and apelike being, similar in appearance to Bigfoot or Sasquatch. Witnesses describe this beast as tall, covered in hair, and having a humanlike shape with long arms. Its fur is typically described as brown, black, or gray. The creature is often reported to stand between 9 feet tall (approximately 2.7 m), making it an imposing and intimidating figure.

The Tennessee Wild Man is believed to be reclusive and elusive, mainly avoiding human contact. It is often reported as a shy and cautious creature, which is why there is limited photographic or concrete evidence of its existence. Reports of sightings of the Tennessee Wild Man date back to the nineteenth century, and they continue to the present day. Witnesses often recount encounters in rural, forested areas. Some have reported hearing eerie and frightening vocalizations that are attributed to the creature. These sounds are often described as howls, screams, or growls. It is said that he is potentially the mortal enemy of the Sasquatch and that they battle for territory. Even if this isn't the case, the legend of the Tennessee Wild Man continues to captivate the imagination of those interested in cryptids and cryptozoology. While there is no definitive proof of its existence, reports of sightings and encounters persist, contributing to the enduring mystery of this perplexing creature.

BIGFOOT

Bigfoot, known colloquially as Sasquatch, occupies a place of mystery and intrigue in the annals of cryptid lore. This legendary creature is said to inhabit the remote and densely wooded expanses of North America, evading humanity's curious gaze while leaving behind tantalizing clues of its existence. Described as a towering figure, Bigfoot stands somewhere between 6 and 10 feet (1.8 and 3 m) in height, possessing a distinctively humanoid or apelike physique adorned with a shaggy coat of hair or fur. Its name, of course, derives from the oversized footprints it occasionally leaves in its wake, marking its elusive presence.

While the enigma of Bigfoot extends far beyond the confines of any specific region, the Appalachian Mountains, with their rugged terrain and vast stretches of wilderness, have garnered a reputation as a potential stronghold for this elusive cryptid. Countless tales and encounters have emerged from within this ancient and storied mountain range, weaving the famous legend of Bigfoot into the fabric of Appalachian folklore.

The Appalachian region, encompassing states such as Tennessee, Kentucky, Virginia, West Virginia, and Pennsylvania, has become a hotbed for reported Bigfoot sightings over the years. Witnesses from these areas have offered a diverse array of descriptions, contributing to the mystique surrounding this elusive creature. Among the many reported variations, one stands out as particularly captivating—a nocturnal Bigfoot distinguished by its coal-black fur and inexplicably eerie, luminescent green eyes.

These sightings, often recounted with awe and trepidation, have left an indelible mark on the collective imagination of the region's inhabitants. The allure of Bigfoot, with its tantalizing blend of the supernatural and the corporeal, continues to captivate those who traverse the winding trails and shadowy recesses of the Appalachian Mountains.

Intriguingly, Bigfoot lore extends far beyond mere sightings and anecdotal accounts. Researchers and enthusiasts have embarked on countless expeditions, armed with cameras, audio recording equipment, and a relentless determination to unveil the secrets of this elusive being. Footprints, hair samples, and even alleged vocalizations have been scrutinized in pursuit of conclusive evidence. Yet, as the years have passed and technology has advanced, Bigfoot remains a cryptid shrouded in mystery.

THE BOOJUM

The Boojum, a mysterious creature in Haywood County, stands at 8 feet tall (2.4 m) and shares similarities with legendary beings like the Abominable Snowman and the Wampus Cat. Covered in thick, gray hair with a less-than-handsome humanlike face, the Boojum is often spotted from a distance on mountain cliffs, emitting haunting moans near hiking trails during twilight. Its elusive home is concealed in the Balsam Mountains, an extension of the Blue Ridge Mountains in southwestern Haywood County.

While tales of the Boojum abound, caution is advised against actively seeking this creature, as stumbling upon it can be frightening, even though it is reputedly harmless unless provoked. The Boojum is known for its interest in pretty girls and precious gemstones found in Western North Carolina. In the early 1900s, stories circulated of women feeling watched while bathing in secluded mountain streams. The Boojum would discreetly observe from beneath the cover of laurels or rhododendron bushes. If it was detected, the startled women would raise alarms, prompting men from the area to hunt the Boojum, though it was never captured.

Presumably retreating to concealed caves in the Balsams, the Boojum safeguarded a trove of gemstones. To protect his jewels, he stored them at the bottom of stone jugs filled with moonshine. If discovered, no mountaineer would waste the coveted liquid; instead, they would consume it, leading to a deep slumber. The Boojum would return and reclaim his gems, leaving the would-be thief with nothing but a throbbing headache upon awakening.

HYBRIDS

Some might assert that a cryptid and a hybrid are the
same thing in the world of cryptozoology, and that
is in a way true. However, the creatures covered in
this section are not attached to any physical evidence
(remember the footprints of Bigfoot, or the slimy tree?).
The Appalachian region is teeming with wildlife, and with
all of the spooky things that go on there, it's not beyond
the scope of reason to assume that some creatures,
when paired with the lore of the area, might have bred
together out of necessity or celestial instruction. Here,
we explore the weird and unexplained. Listen to the
accounts of the witnesses and survivors of these strange
and fearsome sightings and decide for yourself if they
are real. Experience tells me that they are. . .

THE APPALACHIAN BEAR-LION

Imagine, if you will, the dense forests and remote valleys of the Appalachian Mountains, a realm where the ordinary and the extraordinary often blur into one. Here, among the towering trees and babbling brooks, there are stories whispered by those who have encountered the Appalachian Bear-Lion.

This creature is said to be a hybrid, a being that science has yet to fully acknowledge. It's called the Bear-Lion because it's described as a bizarre mish-mash, combining the characteristics of two of the Appalachian's most iconic creatures—the black bear and the mountain lion.

The Appalachian Bear-Lion is known for its immense size, with some accounts claiming it can reach lengths of up to 12 feet (3.7 m) from nose to tail. Its fur is said to be a dark, almost charcoal black, allowing it to blend seamlessly into the shadowy depths of the forests it calls home. But what truly sets it apart is its face, which is said to resemble that of a lion.

This tale was passed down through generations in the Appalachian region—a story of a solitary hunter who ventured deep into the mountains in search of game. This hunter was skilled and fearless, and he had heard the whispers of the Bear-Lion, the creature that was said to possess the strength of a bear and the agility of a mountain lion.

One crisp autumn morning, as the leaves rustled underfoot, the hunter came upon a massive, shadowy figure moving stealthily through the underbrush. It was the Appalachian Bear-Lion, a creature of legend and nightmares. Its eyes gleamed with a sharp intelligence, and its enormous form exuded a sense of primal power.

The hunter, gripped by both fear and fascination, raised his rifle and aimed at the creature. But before he could fire a shot, the Bear-Lion let out a bone-chilling roar that echoed through the mountains, causing the very earth to tremble. It was a roar that seemed to reverberate through time, a sound that spoke of ancient mysteries and untamed wilderness.

Startled and awed, the hunter lowered his weapon, realizing that he stood before a creature that defied explanation. The Bear-Lion regarded him with an inscrutable gaze, and then, with a powerful leap, it vanished into the depths of the forest, leaving the hunter standing alone, humbled, and forever changed by his encounter.

The legend of the Appalachian Bear-Lion endures, a testament to the untamed beauty and unfathomable mysteries of the Appalachian Mountains. Some believe it to be a cryptid, while others see it as a hybridic symbol of the wild and uncharted territories that still exist within the heart of this ancient range.

So, as you explore the Appalachian wilderness, keep your senses sharp and your heart open to the mysteries that dwell within. For you never know when you might come face to face with the legendary and elusive Appalachian Bear-Lion, a creature that bridges the gap between reality and myth.

THE APPALACHIAN CHUPACABRA

There is a legendary hybrid that many think is confined to the southern part of the United States, Mexico, and Puerto Rico, but it has a descendant that is very similar and believed to roam the misty hills and dense forests of West Virginia. Known as the Appalachian Chupacabra, this elusive creature shares its name and some characteristics with its more famous cousin from Latin American folklore, the Chupacabra.

While the origins of the Chupacabra legend are rooted in the warm climates and rural landscapes of places like Puerto Rico and Mexico, the Appalachian Chupacabra has carved out its own niche in the folklore of the Appalachian region of the United States. Here, amid the rolling hills and hidden hollows, tales of encounters with this vampiric cryptid have been whispered for generations, adding an eerie twist to the already mysterious landscape.

The Appalachian Chupacabra is described as a creature of terror and fascination, its appearance steeped in the lore of the region. Witnesses who claim to have encountered this hybrid offer varying yet consistent descriptions, painting a picture of a fearsome entity that strikes dread into the hearts of those who dare to venture into the deep woods.

This creature possesses a lean and muscular frame, suggesting agility and strength. Its body is covered in coarse, dark fur, which blends seamlessly with the shadows of the dense forests it calls home. The fur is often described as matted and unkempt, giving the creature a wild and savage appearance.

The most striking feature of the Appalachian Chupacabra is its head, which resembles a grotesque fusion of canine and reptilian features. Its elongated snout is lined with razor-sharp teeth, capable of tearing through flesh with ease. Glowing amber eyes peer out from beneath a prominent brow ridge, radiating an otherworldly intelligence and malevolence.

Spikes or quills protrude from the creature's back, resembling the spines of a porcupine but thicker and more menacing. These spines are said to bristle when the creature is agitated or on the hunt, serving as a warning to potential prey or adversaries.

Long, sinewy limbs end in clawed paws, each digit tipped with sharp talons capable of rending flesh and gripping prey. It moves with a feline grace, prowling silently through the underbrush as it stalks its next victim.

Despite its fearsome appearance, the Appalachian Chupacabra is said to possess a supernatural allure, drawing unsuspecting travelers deeper into the wilderness with an irresistible curiosity. Its haunting howls and unearthly cries echo through the night, striking fear into the hearts of those who hear them and fueling the legends that surround this monstrous brute.

Sightings have been reported sporadically over the years by residents of the region, which often involve encounters with a strange, unknown creature attacking or killing livestock such as goats, chickens, or other small animals.

Despite its fearsome appearance, the Appalachian Chupacabra is said to possess a supernatural allure, drawing travelers deeper into the wilderness with an irresistible curiosity. Its haunting howls and unearthly cries echo through the night, striking fear into the hearts of those who hear them and fueling the legends that surround this mysterious cryptid.

MONSTERS AND DEMONS

As twilight descends upon the rugged peaks of the Appalachian Mountains, a palpable sense of unease settles over the land like a heavy fog. In the deep, shadowed valleys and dense forests that blanket these ancient hills, whispers of ancient evils and malevolent spirits echo through the darkness. For generations, the people of these remote, isolated communities have whispered tales of strange and otherworldly creatures that roam the hills and hollers under the cover of night. But it is not only the creatures of the night that haunt these ancient hills. For lurking amid the shadows and hidden within the depths of the dense forests, there are whispers of darker, more sinister forces at play. Tales of demonic entities and vengeful spirits, born from the depths of the earth itself, haunt the dreams of those who dare to tread these haunted lands.

MONSTERS

As the moon rises high above the towering peaks and casts its silver light across the landscape, the line between reality and myth begins to blur, and the true nature of the Appalachian mountains is revealed. For in these dark and remote corners of the world, where the veil between the living and the dead is at its thinnest, the spirits of the past still linger, waiting to ensnare the unwary traveler in their web of darkness and despair. Of all the apparitions, haints, and cryptids that roam these haunted hills, the monsters of the region are the most fearsome. While it might be exciting to see a glimpse of the Mothman, or be surprised by a mournful ghost, encountering an Appalachian monster leaves an unmistakable and permanent mark on one's view of the world.

THE GRAFTON MONSTER

One silent and foggy morning in 1964, the residents of Grafton, West Virginia, woke to the invigorating smells of coffee and toast and sat at their breakfast tables to start the day. But today was a bit different as newspapers were unfolded to reveal the front-page headline declaring that a real-life monster had been seen in town. The article, written by Robert Cockrell, claimed that along a desolate stretch of Route 119, along the Tygart Valley River, lurked a monster so scary, so threatening, it could make blood run icy cold. Epically tall and with skin as smooth as a baby seal, it appeared to be missing its head. But that didn't stop it from producing a trill whistle that pierced the night and ears, a markedly alien sound. In the article, Cockrell had no idea that he was making history when he coined the terrifying beast the Graftan Monster. Now also known as the "Grafton Creature" or "West Virginia Bigfoot," this beast is considered to be one of the scariest in all of Appalachian history.

Since then, the sightings have seemingly slowed but certainly not stopped. Most perplexing, though, is that every person who has encountered this strange creature has reported that they got the sense that it was somehow from another universe—as in, an actual alien. And if that is the case, then what is it doing here? What is it trying to say with its shrill, ear-shattering whistle? Some believe a Grafton Monster sighting is a warning of the worst kind of personal bad news, while others claim its manifestation and piercing shriek to be an intergalactic message for all of humanity. And others yet think it's simply a mutation of a bear or Sasquatch. But then where is its head?

THE APPALACHIAN SILVER GIANT

The Appalachian Silver Giant is a colossal humanoid creature intimately ingrained in the folklore of the Appalachian region. Described as an imposing figure that can run on two legs as easily as it can four, it is said to stand nearly 10 feet (3 m) tall, with a robust frame weighing over 500 pounds (227 kg). The creature is distinguished by its shaggy silver fur, a distinctive feature that lends it an aura of otherworldly mystique. Is it a ghostly apparition of a bear—one that can rip out the throats of its enemies? Is it a Sasquatch, its eyes rumored to glow eerily in the dark, adding to its imposing presence? What is known for sure is that it lurks deep in the southern woodland and crossing this beast's path is only for the foolhardy.

The Silver Giant is often depicted as a solitary predator that roams the mountains and forests of the region. Its dietary preferences are said to encompass a range of prey, including livestock, wildlife, and, in chilling accounts, the occasional person without discretion for young or old. The creature's immense strength and agility render it a formidable adversary, leaving those who cross its path with vivid and unsettling images of their lives flashing before their eyes in sheer terror.

The Silver Giant's fearsome reputation has ingrained it in the culture of the region as a creature to be regarded with all of the caution and mistrust one can muster. It has become an omen of impending doom or tragedy in the eyes of many. Local legends often allude to the necessity of powerful magic or divine intervention to overcome this imposing monster and banish it from lurking on the outskirts of their communities in an effort to avoid any bad luck or tragedy, but also for the simple fact of avoiding becoming its prey.

Interestingly, the genesis of the Silver Giant is relatively recent, with its roots traced back to the mid-twentieth century. Some speculations suggest it could be a previously undiscovered primate species, as if a mere human had genetically morphed into the monstrous creature that now lurks in the area today. Whether you believe in it or not, just don't look it in the eyes when you do finally encounter it.

THE FLATWOODS MONSTER

The Flatwoods Monster, also known as the Braxton County Monster, Braxie, the Green Monster, or the Phantom of Flatwoods, is one of the most perplexing and enduring mysteries in the realm of American monsters. This eerie and otherworldly creature allegedly made its first appearance in the small town of Flatwoods, West Virginia, in 1952. Over the years, it has become an icon of Appalachian folklore and a symbol of the unexplained.

The story of the Flatwoods Monster begins on the evening of September 12, 1952, when a group of local children, led by brothers Edward and Fred May, claimed to have witnessed a bizarre and terrifying sight. As the group played in the yard, they reported seeing a bright, pulsating object streak across the sky and crash on the nearby Fisher Farm.

Fueled by curiosity and a sense of adventure, the children, accompanied by Edward's mother, Kathleen May, and another local teenager, Eugene Lemon, embarked on a journey to investigate the crash site. Armed with flashlights, they set out for the farm, where they expected to find a downed airplane.

Upon arriving at the location, their excitement turned to sheer terror. Instead of an aircraft, they encountered a monstrous figure, standing at an imposing 10 feet (3 m) tall, with a dark, shadowy silhouette. The creature was described as having a face dominated by glowing, reddish-orange eyes, a metallic, nonhuman body, and long, spindly, clawlike appendages. The entity emitted a hissing noise and a nauseating mist that enveloped the witnesses, causing some to experience symptoms of sickness.

Word of the Flatwoods Monster encounter quickly spread throughout the region, attracting media attention, and piquing the interest of investigators. A local newspaper, the Braxton Democrat, covered the incident extensively, coining the term "Monster" to describe the mysterious entity.

US authorities and military personnel also arrived to examine the area, though no official explanation was ever provided. The incident was classified as a UFO encounter, but there is no definitive physical evidence that an extraterrestrial craft was found. In fact, all that really appeared to confirm that anything that had landed there was skid marks across the field. Witnesses, including the children and Kathleen May, maintained their accounts of the encounter.

As with many UFO-related phenomena, there are various theories attempting to explain the Flatwoods Monster encounter. Skeptics suggest that the incident was the result of a meteorite or falling debris, while others propose that it could have been an elaborate hoax or a case of mass hysteria. Some ufologists and paranormal enthusiasts believe that the Flatwoods Monster was indeed an extraterrestrial being, potentially associated with the UFO sighting reported by the witnesses. Others speculate that it might have been a creature not yet identified by science.

The Flatwoods Monster remains a tantalizing and unexplained mystery, continuing to captivate the imagination of those intrigued by the uncharted realms of cryptids and UFO encounters.

THE WENDIGO

In the depths of the Appalachian Mountains, where the dense forests guard age-old mysteries and the wind wails mournfully through the hollows, dwells a creature of insatiable hunger and ceaseless dread: the Wendigo. Steeped in the chilling lore of Native American tribes across North America, the Wendigo embodies the darkest depths of human desperation and an insatiable thirst for flesh that drives it to unspeakable acts of horror.

The legend of the Wendigo traces its roots back to the Algonquian-speaking tribes of the northeastern United States and Canada, including those who once called the Appalachian region home. According to Indigenous folklore, the Wendigo is a malevolent spirit born from the depths of the wilderness, embodying the insatiable greed and cannibalistic desires of those who succumb to its influence. It is said to be a cursed being, transformed from a human into a monstrous creature driven by an unending hunger for human flesh.

Described as towering and emaciated, with sunken eyes that burn with an otherworldly fire, the Wendigo cuts a terrifying figure against the backdrop of the forest. Its skin, stretched tight over protruding bones, is pallid and ashen, reflecting the chill of the grave. Long, gnarled claws extend from its skeletal hands, ready to rend and tear at its prey, while its gaping maw drips with the ichor of its victims.

The Wendigo is a creature of primal instinct and unfathomable cruelty, driven by a hunger that knows no bounds. Those who encounter one are said to be consumed by madness, driven to acts of unspeakable violence and depravity as they give in to the creature's corrupting influence.

Reports of sightings and encounters with the Wendigo are rare but chilling, often recounted in hushed tones around campfires and hearths deep in the Appalachian Mountains. Some claim to have heard its petrifying cries echoing through the night, while others speak of fleeting glimpses of its shadowy form stalking through the trees. Though skeptics dismiss such tales as the products of overactive imaginations or the hallucinations of weary travelers, those who have felt the icy grip of fear that accompanies the Wendigo's presence know better than to dismiss its existence out of hand.

The Wendigo's presence in popular culture has deeply influenced the folklore of the Appalachian region, weaving its way into the fabric of stories, literature, and media that capture the imagination of audiences worldwide. From novels and short stories by authors such as Algernon Blackwood and Stephen King to films, television shows, and video games, the Wendigo has become an iconic figure in horror and supernatural genres. Its depiction as a malevolent force of nature, driven by insatiable hunger and primal instinct, has cemented its status as one of the most terrifying creatures in folklore.

DEMONS

Demons have been a subject of much debate spanning geography and time. Nearly every culture on earth has at least one demonic-type entity and they are most often tied to religious and cultural beliefs. They are spiritual beings that are no less than malevolent and dangerous, not only to your physical body, but also to your very soul. Accounts of demon sightings and encounters have terrified the Appalachian community for centuries and it hasn't slowed down. Many Appalachian superstitions are based on preventing these evil beings from infecting your life by bringing disease, destruction, and deep misfortune. Folk magic, granny magic, and elements of Christianity empower the residents of this region in warding off and protecting themselves from these nasty and dark forces. By far the darkest of all the creatures in this book, demons can be terrifying to encounter, and at times, difficult to rid yourself from their influence. I suggest you revisit the protection charm from chapter two before diving in to this frightening section.

THE JERSEY DEVIL

The Jersey Devil is a legendary creature said to inhabit the Pine Barrens of southern New Jersey. Described as a winged, hooved, and generally demonic entity, the legend of the Jersey Devil has been a prominent part of New Jersey folklore for centuries.

The creature's origin is often traced back to a woman named Mother Leeds, who, according to the legend, was frustrated upon learning that she was pregnant with her thirteenth child. In exasperation, she exclaimed that the child might as well be the devil. When the child was born, it is said to have transformed into a hideous creature with bat-like wings, a horse's head, and hooves. The Jersey Devil as an entity is often described as a creature with leathery wings, a long neck, and a forked tail. It is said to emit a blood-curdling scream or howl, contributing to its reputation as a harbinger of bad luck and doom.

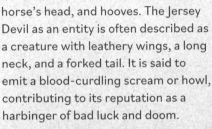

The legend of the Jersey Devil has become deeply ingrained in New Jersey culture, inspiring various stories, books, and even a hockey team mascot. The creature's notoriety has extended beyond folklore, with some attributing mysterious occurrences and strange events in the Pine Barrens to the presence of the legendary Jersey Devil.

THE DOVER DEMON

In the quiet town of Dover, Massachusetts, nestled among the trees and winding roads, a mysterious legend was born in the spring of 1977—the legend of the Dover Demon.

It all began on a chilling night when three teenagers, Bill Bartlett, Mike Mazzocca, and Andy Brodie, set out for a drive. Little did they know that their journey would lead them to an encounter that defied explanation. As they cruised through the darkness, a peculiar figure emerged before them—a small, humanoid creature with a watermelon-shaped head and eyes that glowed like orbs in the night.

Bill Bartlett, the first to witness this strange being, was so captivated—or perhaps terrified—by the sight that he later sketched the creature, giving life to the now-iconic image of the Dover Demon. News of their bizarre encounter spread through the town like wildfire.

The next evening another teenager, John Baxter, ventured into the night, unsuspecting that his walk home would thrust him into the heart of the Dover Demon mystery. Just like Bill and his friends, John saw the creature—a small, unearthly being with a large head and eyes that seemed to pierce through the darkness. The sightings puzzled the townsfolk and ignited the imaginations of those far beyond the town's borders. The Dover Demon, with its peach-colored skin, spindly frame, and long, tendril-like fingers, became a cryptic enigma that captured the attention of both the curious and the skeptical.

As the tale unfolded, skeptics posited rational explanations. Could the witnesses have mistaken a known animal for the Dover Demon? Perhaps a young moose or an owl played a role in the sightings. Some even questioned if it was a shared hallucination or an elaborate prank. Yet, despite the attempts at debunking it, the legend of the Dover Demon persists. The mysterious creature, with its glowing eyes and peculiar appearance, became an enduring and beloved part of Appalachian lore.

THE SQUONK

In the dense and mysterious forests of Pennsylvania, there exists a monster steeped in sadness and draped in its own unique legend: the Squonk.

The tale of the Squonk unfolds in the darkened woods, where the creature is said to dwell, hidden away from prying eyes. Described as a grotesque and sorrowful being, the Squonk is burdened by a singular affliction—it cannot bear to face its reflection. It even disgusts itself, with its scaly skin hanging in loose folds about its body, covered from head to toe in warts and blemishes.

The Squonk is said to be perpetually unhappy with its appearance, and this discontent is its tragic flaw. Unable to find solace within its own skin, the creature weeps silently in the shadows, wandering through the secluded woodlands of Pennsylvania.

Legend has it that those who venture into the forest, hoping to catch a glimpse of the elusive Squonk, will likely never succeed. The demon, burdened by its self-loathing, hides away from the world, making it nearly impossible to find. However, there are whispers of a unique strategy employed by those daring enough to seek the Squonk.

The legend suggests that the Squonk's vulnerability lies in its propensity to dissolve into a pool of tears when cornered or captured. Some intrepid hunters have tried to capture the creature by setting out mirrors in the forest. These mirrors lure the Squonk with the cruel promise of seeing its own reflection, exploiting its deep-seated desire for acceptance. Though repelled by its own appearance, the Squonk is irresistibly drawn to the mirrors, hoping to find some form of validation. When it sees its reflection, the overwhelming self-loathing and despair cause it to dissolve into tears, leaving behind only a damp trail as evidence of its presence. This tragic interaction highlights the Squonk's internal conflict, as it is both attracted to and repelled by its own image, forever seeking the acceptance it believes it lacks.

THE APPALACHIAN DEVIL

Within the dim valleys and rugged summits of the Appalachian Mountains, the Devil's presence is pronounced, surpassing the boundaries of conventional religious doctrine to embody a complex and mysterious figure intricately intertwined with the region's folklore. Unlike the straightforward depiction of evil portrayed in Bible stories, the Appalachian Devil assumes a variety of guises and functions, mirroring the diverse cultural influences that have contributed to the intricate mosaic of local beliefs and superstitions.

Unlike tales that depict selling one's soul to the Devil for wealth and fame, this aspect of Appalachian folklore presents a different narrative. Here, the Devil is said to offer knowledge, talent, and power in exchange for a pact made at the crossroads. This belief spawned superstitions surrounding the fiddle, which was kept outside homes to avoid bad luck, drawing from legends of musicians making deals with the Devil at crossroads.

Furthermore, from the Indigenous peoples who first inhabited the area to the European settlers who later arrived, Appalachia has been home to a diverse array of cultural traditions and beliefs. These influences are reflected in the region's folklore, where elements of Native American, African, and European mythology converge to create a unique and distinctly Appalachian interpretation of the Devil. For example, among the Cherokee people, the Devil is known as "The Black Man," a malevolent spirit associated with disease and death. This characterization reflects the Cherokee view of the Devil as a powerful and fearsome figure who wields influence over the forces of nature.

Similarly, African influences depict the Devil as a cunning trickster who brings both good and bad fortune to those he

encounters, reflecting the complex relationship between humans and the supernatural world. And the European influence can plainly be seen in the Christian imagery that typically follows these tales.

Another notable aspect of the Appalachian Devil is its role as a guardian of tradition and morality. While the Devil is often portrayed as a figure of temptation and corruption,

Appalachian folklore also depicts the Devil as a moral arbiter who punishes those who stray from the path of righteousness. This is evident in stories where the Devil appears to challenge individuals to prove their virtue or test their faith, serving as a cautionary tale against moral laxity and spiritual complacency.

The Appalachian view of the Devil also shares some commonalities with the broader global perception of this entity. Like their counterparts around the world, Appalachian residents often invoke the Devil as a scapegoat for misfortune or as a symbol of temptation and sin. Moreover, the Devil's association with themes of temptation, corruption, and moral ambiguity resonates across cultures, reflecting universal aspects of the human experience.

Numerous folktales illustrate the Devil's presence in Appalachian folklore. One might report encountering a shadowy figure resembling a goat, while another might tell of coming across a drunken man wrestling with a mysterious assailant on a mountain path. Other reports involve fiddlers playing for dancing crowds, only to realize they've been entertaining the Devil himself.

Despite his sinister reputation, some tales portray the Devil in a more nuanced light, showing acts of kindness or compassion. Whether a symbol of temptation or a metaphor for life's trials, the Appalachian Devil remains a central figure in the region's folklore, embodying the struggles and resilience of its people across generations.

THE RAVEN MOCKER

The Cherokee Nation of the Appalachians has long held sacred beliefs and stories that are woven into the fabric of their culture. Among these tales stands the legend of the Raven Mocker, a mysterious and frightening figure. This guardian of the sacred realm is both feared and revered, representing the Cherokee's devoted connection to the spiritual world and their ancestral lands.

The Raven Mocker, or "Kâ'lanû Ahkyeli'skï," in Cherokee, meaning "the one that robs a dying man of life," is a malevolent entity in Cherokee folklore. According to tradition, the Raven Mocker is a malevolent witch who gains power and longevity by consuming the hearts of the dying.

The Raven Mocker is said to be a grotesque, emaciated figure, often depicted as a wizened old man or woman. They are typically covered in dark feathers or a shadowy shroud, their eyes glowing with an unnatural fire. In some versions of the legend, they are described as having talon-like hands and elongated, skeletal fingers, ideal for reaching into the chests of the dying.

The primary role of the Raven Mocker is to extract the souls of the dying. Cherokee beliefs hold that the soul must be set free to ensure a peaceful journey to the afterlife. However, the Raven Mocker's intentions are far from benevolent. They are driven by an evil hunger for power, often preying upon those who have accumulated great wealth or wisdom in their lifetime. These sinister entities lurk in the shadows, listening for the telltale signs of death, such as the cries of a mourning family.

One of the most feared aspects of the Raven Mocker is their eerie cry, which is said to be heard in the wind just before someone's passing. This cry is an omen of death, and Cherokee elders warn that when you hear it, you should take extra precautions to protect your loved ones.

While the Raven Mocker is typically portrayed as a baleful figure, it also serves as a guardian of Cherokee traditions and values. The fear of encountering a Raven Mocker is a reminder to live a virtuous life and to respect the spiritual world. In Cherokee culture, death is seen as a transition rather than an end, and the Raven Mocker underscores the importance of this belief.

To ward off the Raven Mocker, Cherokee tradition offers various protective measures. These superstitions include placing knives, scissors, or other sharp objects beneath the bed of a dying person, as the Raven Mocker is believed to fear these objects. Additionally, chanting sacred songs and prayers can help protect the soul of the departed.

The Raven Mocker is a complex and compelling figure in Cherokee folklore, representing the duality of life and death, good and evil. While their malevolent nature is feared, they also serve as a reminder of the importance of Cherokee spirituality, tradition, and the enduring connection between the living and the spirit world.

THE DEVIL MONKEY

Reports of an unusual creature in Saltville, Virginia, have sparked intrigue and speculation for years. Described as a unique species of monkey-like creature, these sightings have left witnesses both bewildered and cautious. Terrified witnesses have offered varying descriptions of the Devil Monkey, with some claiming it stands at a height of about 4 feet (1.2 m), while others insist it can reach heights exceeding 7 feet (2 m). However, it is important to note that the larger version of this creature appears to resemble a humanoid more than the smaller, primate-like Devil Monkey.

Saltville, located in Smyth County, Virginia, is not only historically known for its role as a source of salt for early settlers and the Confederacy but has also gained notoriety due to sightings of the mysterious Devil Monkey.

The legend of the Devil Monkey in Saltville is said to have begun in 1959 when a couple was driving near the town. Suddenly, they were confronted by a large, apelike creature that aggressively attacked their car, leaving scratch marks. According to the couple's daughter, the creature had "light, taffy-colored hair" with a white blaze on its neck and underbelly. It stood on two powerful hind legs and had shorter front limbs.

A few years later, two Saltville nurses driving home from work in the early morning hours experienced a similar encounter with the Devil Monkey. Once again, the creature attacked their car, tearing off the convertible top. Fortunately, no one was harmed during these incidents.

In 1994, a woman from Ohio traveling through South West Virginia in the Roanoke area had a chilling encounter with a creature that would add to the Devil Monkey lore. While driving on a remote two-lane road south of Roanoke, around 2:30 a.m., a creature leaped across the road in front of her car. This creature was described as a monkey-wolf hybrid, covered in short, sleek black fur. It stood at approximately 6 feet tall (1.8 m) on its hind legs and possessed pointy ears, a flat snout, and a long, thin tail. The creature was noted for its muscular and slender physique.

Following this sighting, stories emerged of missing pets and livestock in the area. Additionally, more sightings of the mysterious creature were reported, causing unease among the local population.

THE SMOKE WOLF

The Appalachian Smoke Wolf is a legendary and evasive predator known for its nocturnal hunting habits, targeting livestock, wildlife, and occasionally humans who cross its path. Those who claim to have seen it describe it as resembling a large, wolflike creature with black fur and striking red eyes, reminiscent of the classic tale of Little Red Riding Hood.

One of the most distinctive features of the Smoke Wolf is its ability to transform into a cloud of smoke, rendering it nearly impossible to track or capture. Additionally, the creature can only be deterred by the sound of rattling chains, which some believe to be its weakness. When the Smoke Wolf vocalizes, it's described as emitting a chilling howl resembling a wolf's cry combined with the scream of a demon.

The legend of the Smoke Wolf is relatively recent, dating back to the early 1900s when reports of a mysterious, smokelike creature began circulating in the Appalachian region. Some speculated that it might be a supernatural entity or an undiscovered species of wolf.

The Smoke Wolf's unique characteristics, supernatural abilities, and frightening howl make it a compelling addition to the eclectic canon of Appalachian folklore.

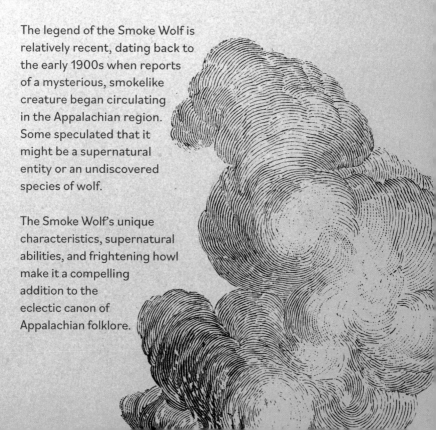

SPEARFINGER

In Cherokee folklore, Spearfinger, also known as U'tlun'ta, is a malevolent and legendary figure who has been a source of both fear and caution for generations. This shape-shifting witch, said to reside in the Smoky Mountains of North Carolina and Tennessee, is renowned for her insatiable appetite for human livers and her sinister tactics to deceive and harm those who cross her path.

Spearfinger is described as a haggard, elderly woman with stone feet, and a single, long, bony, spear-like finger on her right hand, which she uses to slice open her victims and extract their livers. Her skin is said to be as hard as stone, making her virtually invulnerable to attack. What makes Spearfinger particularly fearsome is her ability to shape-shift, allowing her to assume various forms, making her a cunning and elusive antagonist. Spearfinger's modus operandi involves disguising herself as a kind, geriatric, and unassuming woman to gain the trust of her victims, especially young children. Once she has lured them into her confidence, she uses her sharp finger to extract their livers, often while they are asleep. To avoid detection, she leaves no trace of her sinister deeds, as her victims typically die painlessly and in silence.

The Cherokee people highly valued chestnuts as a vital source of nourishment. During the autumn season, there was a tradition of igniting large brush fires to roast chestnuts in a designated area, ensuring a bountiful supply for the harsh winter months. However, these blazing fires unwittingly drew the attention of Spearfinger, a malevolent entity with a relentless appetite. She would lurk in the vicinity, preying on stragglers and individuals who momentarily strayed alone away from the group's safety.

When darkness descended, Spearfinger would shroud herself in the guise of an old lady, appearing in Cherokee villages under

the pretense of needing assistance. Gaining the trust of unsuspecting village children, she would bide her time until they succumbed to sleep, at which point she would claim them as her victims. On occasion, Spearfinger would assume the form of her most recent child victim, returning to their dwelling. There, she would patiently await the slumber of the family and proceed to harvest their livers.

Cherokee hunters recounted sinister tales of encountering decrepit women in the woods, singing haunting melodies as a prelude to their malevolent deeds. Legend has it that Spearfinger, a fearsome witch, preferred attacking from behind, using her elongated, razor-sharp finger, which was about as long as a spear, to pierce her victims' necks. This deadly finger could reach their hearts before she extracted their livers. In response to this dire threat, the Cherokee community rallied together to devise a trap for Spearfinger. While they remained uncertain about how to permanently defeat her, they resolved to address that challenge once she was contained.

Their trap consisted of digging a concealed pit, camouflaged with brush, designed to ensnare her. Then, the Cherokee set ablaze one of their immense brush fires, a beacon meant to lure her closer. True to their expectations, she descended from Chilhowee Mountain in pursuit of the fire's source. The resonating thunder of her stone footsteps echoed ominously across the land.

As Spearfinger neared the group of hunters stationed near the village, she feigned distress, calling out for help. However, they remained steadfast, no longer deceived by her tricks. A well-aimed spear struck her square in the chest, though it splintered upon impact. A barrage of arrows followed, but they merely glanced off Spearfinger's stone-like exterior.

Undeterred, Spearfinger surged forward, revealing her deadly right hand and spear-finger. As she continued to deflect the hunters' arrows, she stumbled into the concealed pit, unable to free herself. Within the pit, she lashed out in a frenzy, attempting to harm her captors with her razor finger, all the while maintaining her frightening song.

A pivotal moment occurred when a chickadee landed on Spearfinger's right hand, diverting her attention. Seizing this opportunity, the hunters closed in, attacking her right hand and severing it, revealing her concealed heart. With the destruction of her hidden heart, Spearfinger's malevolence was finally thwarted.

Though the Cherokee claimed victory over Spearfinger, the legend endures, passed down through generations, whispered as if she might still linger in the shadows. The legend is closely associated with the rugged and hauntingly beautiful landscape of the Great Smoky Mountains, which straddle the border of North Carolina and Tennessee, and it is within these dense forests and rolling hills that Spearfinger is believed to reside. Her presence serves as a stark reminder to those who venture into the wilderness to exercise caution and respect for the natural world.

THE DEVIL'S TRAMPING GROUND

 The Devil's Tramping Ground is a mysterious and creepy phenomenon located in a forested area near Harper's Crossroads in Bear Creek, North Carolina. It is a roughly circular patch of land about 40 feet (12 m) in diameter, where no vegetation grows. The area is characterized by a lack of plant life, and legend has it that anything placed within the circle overnight will be removed or destroyed by morning.

Local folklore and legends surrounding the Devil's Tramping Ground have been passed down through generations. The most common legend suggests that the Devil himself paces in a circle at night, plotting evil deeds. According to the legend, nothing grows in the circle because the Devil's presence prevents any plant life from thriving.

Various stories and accounts describe strange occurrences in the vicinity of the Devil's Tramping Ground. Some claim to have witnessed bizarre lights or experienced unusual phenomena, adding to the mystique of the site. The area has become a subject of fascination for those interested in the supernatural, and it has attracted curious visitors and paranormal enthusiasts.

THE WOOD BOOGER

Appalachian people have passed down tales of the Wood Booger for generations. This elusive creature—sometimes known as the Sasquatch of the South or the Eastern Bigfoot—is said to be a towering, shaggy behemoth that roams the wilderness under the cover of night.

Now, the Wood Booger is not your typical campfire tale. No, my friends, it's a legend that has been whispered by hunters, hikers, and folks who call these mountains home. It's a legend rooted in both fear and fascination, for those who have glimpsed this creature say it's like nothing they've ever seen.

The Wood Booger, you see, stands at least 8 feet (2.4 m) tall, with matted, fur-covered skin that ranges from dark brown to a mottled gray. Its shoulders are broad, and its arms dangle down past its knees, each limb ending in long, gnarled fingers that could easily wrap around a man's throat. Its face—well, that's the stuff of nightmares, with large, piercing eyes that gleam in the moonlight and a wide, lipless mouth filled with jagged, yellowed teeth.

Now, I should tell you, the Wood Booger isn't known for being particularly aggressive, but it's fiercely territorial. It's said to dwell deep in the heart of the Appalachian wilderness, far from the prying eyes of humanity. And woe betide anyone who stumbles upon its lair or threatens its domain.

Many a hunter has ventured into these woods, tracking game, and hoping for a prized trophy, only to come face to face with the piercing gaze of the Wood Booger. They tell tales of feeling a chill run down their spine as the creature watches them from the shadows, its eyes never leaving their form. Some claim to

have heard eerie, guttural cries echoing through the trees, as if the Wood Booger is warning them to stay away.

But for all its fearsome reputation, the Wood Booger has also been known to display a curious and mischievous side. Stories abound of hikers and campers waking up to find their gear mysteriously rearranged or missing, as if the creature has been playing tricks on them in the dead of night.

And then there are the tales of folks who've ventured into the wilderness with nothing but a camera and a sense of adventure, hoping to catch a glimpse of this elusive creature. Some have returned with blurry photographs and shaky video footage, evidence that only serves to stoke the flames of the legend.

THE APPALACHIAN BLACK PANTHER

Picture yourself venturing into the darkness of night, stumbling upon a formidable creature, its pitch-black fur akin to the midnight sky. This demonic beast possesses piercing yellow eyes, and its formidable fangs strike terror into the hearts of all who encounter it. The pioneers and early settlers of the Appalachian region have passed down tales of these elusive black panthers, stealthy predators prowling the nocturnal wilderness. Despite the skepticism of contemporary wildlife experts, no photographic evidence or captures of these creatures exist in recent times. Nevertheless, these legends persist within the heart of the Appalachians and the Ozarks, where the mysterious continues to captivate the imagination.

Historical accounts even recount Texan residents bearing witness to these shadowy creatures during the 1800s, further fueling the notion that these demon-panthers could have maintained a hidden existence in the deep recesses of the Appalachian Mountains.

Delving into the annals of Montgomery County, Arkansas' history unveils a gripping black panther encounter. In the quietude of her home, Emily Stacy found herself alone with her children when a ferocious and untamed presence manifested. This untamed entity relentlessly assailed her front door, endeavoring to breach the sanctity of her home. Not one to yield to fear, Emily exhibited remarkable courage. She loaded her musket, her hands unwavering, and steadied herself for the impending confrontation. She took aim and fired a shot through the wooden door. When dawn broke, the porch bore witness to a lifeless black panther, often described as a black mountain lion, a chilling legend that has endured the test of time.

THE APPALACHIAN TRAIL MURDERS

In the early 1980s, as spring blossomed across the Pennsylvania section of the trail, a monster in his own right named Randall Lee Smith emerged from the shadows. A drifter with a troubled past, Smith's malevolence would soon shatter the peace of the trail. Two unsuspecting hikers, Robert Mountford Jr. and Laura Ramsay, became entangled in his web of violence in the Shingletown Gap area.

Under the leafy canopy of the forest, Smith, armed with a knife and fueled by malevolent intent, attacked the hikers. The air was filled with the desperate cries of the victims as Smith's blade struck, leaving Mountford lifeless and Ramsay severely injured. In the aftermath, Smith vanished into the woods, leaving a trail of terror behind.

Justice would eventually catch up with the possessed assailant as he was captured and faced the consequences of his heinous deeds. The tragic incident prompted reflections on safety along the trail, a sacred space meant for self-discovery and communion with nature.

Years later, the Appalachian Trail found itself marred by another dark episode. In the spring of 2019, a man named James Jordan, also known as Sovereign, stalked the verdant paths of Virginia. His erratic behavior and menacing presence foreshadowed a dreadful encounter with a group of unsuspecting hikers.

As the sun dipped below the tree-lined horizon, Jordan's confrontation with the hikers took a gruesome turn. In the heart of the wilderness, a life was taken, and the echoes of violence reverberated through the trees. Ronald Sanchez Jr. fell victim to the demonic force that was Sovereign, while another hiker suffered injuries in the chaos.

The Appalachian Trail, once a symbol of freedom and communion with nature, now bore witness to the darker facets of human nature. Authorities swiftly pursued Jordan, who attempted to elude justice by disappearing into the forest he had turned into a crime scene.

These tales, though tragic, stand as stark reminders that even in the sanctuary of nature, darkness can intrude. Yet, for every grim story, countless others unfold along the Appalachian Trail—stories of resilience, camaraderie, and the enduring spirit of those who seek solace in the embrace of the mountains. The trail, with its winding paths and hidden wonders, continues to draw in adventurers, inspiring them to face the unknown and find strength within themselves.

THE PUCKWUDGIE

The Puckwudgie is a mythical demon from Native American folklore, particularly associated with the Wampanoag and Algonquian tribes of the northeastern United States, including areas within the Appalachian region. Described as small humanoid beings, Puckwudgies are said to possess a variety of magical abilities and are often considered mischievous or even malevolent entities.

Standing at an uncertain height, their forms cloaked in darkness, Pukwudgies are shrouded in mystery. Some speak of knee-high demonic creatures that move with an otherworldly grace, their smooth, gray skin often glowing with an eerie luminescence, casting a pallid light upon the dense undergrowth that conceals their presence.

With large, pointed ears and bulbous noses, Pukwudgies possess a visage that inspires dread in those who dare to gaze upon them. Glowing red eyes, like smoldering embers in the night, pierce through the darkness, marking them as creatures of unearthly origin. Some witnesses speak of fur-covered forms, with noses akin to wolves and glowing eyes that burn with an intensity that chills the soul.

Despite their diminutive stature, Pukwudgies possess formidable powers that make them a force to be reckoned with. They can appear and disappear at will, confounding the senses and leading unsuspecting travelers astray in the wilderness. Their magical abilities are vast and varied, ranging from the ability to create fire and launch poison arrows to shapeshifting into dangerous animals or assuming a hybrid form that is half-human, half-porcupine.

But beware, for crossing paths with a Pukwudgie is a perilous proposition. These mischievous beings delight in tormenting humans, whether through cunning tricks or deadly attacks. Those who dare to annoy them may find themselves stalked by the creature, their memories forgotten, or their lives cut short by a swift and deadly strike. Some speak of kidnappings, of children spirited away into the depths of the forest, never to be seen again. Others tell of harrowing encounters with sand that blinds and knives that cut deep, leaving behind scars both physical and psychological.

Legend has it that the animosity between Pukwudgies and humans dates back to ancient times, rooted in a conflict between the Wampanoag tribe and the creatures they deemed a nuisance. Maushop the giant, beloved by the tribe, cast the Pukwudgies out of the land, their resentment simmering beneath the surface for generations to come.

The origins of the Puckwudgie legend can be traced back to the Native American peoples of the northeastern United States, particularly the Wampanoag and Algonquian tribes. Puckwudgies are often associated with sacred places in the wilderness and are believed to be spirits of the forest. Over time, the legend of the Puckwudgie has become intertwined with the broader folklore of the Appalachian region, where sightings and encounters with these mysterious beings continue to be reported.

GRIMS

In the shadowy hills of the Appalachian Mountains dwell the mysterious guardians known as Grims. These beings are said to stand vigil over certain cemeteries scattered throughout the region, their red eyes piercing the veil between the living and the dead. Legend has it that settlers in the Appalachian region held a belief so profound that it transcended the boundaries of life and death: burying the family dog alive in a cemetery would ensure the dog's spirit would transform into a Grim, a formidable demon-like protector of the graves.

The origins of the Grim are shrouded in time, entwined with Appalachian oral traditions. Belief in these spectral guardians persists, passed down through generations via whispered tales and enduring superstitions. According to folklore, burying a beloved dog alive in a cemetery formed a solemn pact, forging a sacred bond between humans and animals that transcended death. In return for this sacrifice, it was believed the dog's spirit would transform into a Grim, tasked with guarding the graves of the departed.

The Grims themselves are described as formidable creatures, with sleek black fur that seems to absorb the moonlight, rendering them invisible in the darkness of the night. Their eyes, however, burn like fiery coals, casting an eerie glow that strikes fear into the hearts of any who dares to trespass upon their domain. Some tales speak of Grims with teeth as sharp as razors and claws that can rend flesh from bone, while others describe them as spectral whisps that drift silently through the graveyard, unseen and untouched by mortal hands.

Despite their fearsome appearance, Grims can be malevolent beings, but are also seen as guardians of the dead, bound by ancient oaths to protect the sanctity of the cemetery. It is said that they will fiercely defend the graves under their watch, driving away any who would desecrate or disturb the resting places of the departed. Yet, they are also creatures of great sorrow, haunted by the memories of their former lives and the sacrifices they made to become Grims.

Reports of sightings of Grims are rare but chilling, often recounted by those who claim to have ventured into the depths of the Appalachian wilderness in search of these legendary beings. Some speak of encounters with shadowy figures that lurk among the tombstones, their red eyes gleaming in the darkness like beacons of warning. Others tell of eerie howls that echo through the night, signaling the presence of a Grim nearby. Though skeptics may dismiss such tales as the products of overactive imaginations or the effects of moonlit shadows, those who have felt the icy grip of fear that accompanies an encounter with a Grim know better than to dismiss their existence.

In the tapestry of Appalachian folklore, the Grims occupy a unique and haunting place, weaving their way through the tales and legends that have shaped the cultural landscape of the region for centuries. As long as the mountains stand and the wind whispers through the trees, the Grims will continue to stand watch over the cemeteries of Appalachia, their red eyes burning bright in the darkness, a silent testament to the enduring power of myth and legend.

THE APPALACHIAN TUNNELS

The legend of the Appalachian Tunnels involves mysterious underground passageways along the Appalachian Trail. Many of the legends trace back to a secret military base, hidden away in the Blue Ridge Summit. According to the tales, the military was conducting experiments of an otherworldly nature in underground labs. The exact nature of these experiments is often left to the imagination, but the common theme is that something went awry.

The crux of the stories involves beings created through these experiments, not quite human but possessing powers or characteristics beyond the natural. Whether they were the result of genetic manipulation, supernatural forces, or a combination of both, these beings are said to have broken free from their confines and sought refuge in the Appalachian wilderness.

The escapees are rumored to have found shelter in a network of secret underground tunnels, believed to run beneath the Appalachian Trail. These tunnels, remnants of the military base or natural formations, become the backdrop for encounters between the mysterious beings and unsuspecting travelers.

Hikers and locals claim to have glimpsed these mysterious beings. Descriptions vary, with some accounts portraying them as protectors of the mountains, while others paint a more ominous picture. Sightings of these gruesome murders often occur near or within the alleged tunnels, adding an air of suspense to the tales.

The legends diverge on the nature of these tunnel-dwellers. Some stories suggest they act as guardians, watching over the mountains and their secrets. In contrast, darker versions

warn of malevolent entities, perhaps keeping the secrets of the tunnels locked away from prying eyes.

The tunnels are said to echo with strange sounds—whispers, footsteps, or otherworldly noises. These auditory phenomena contribute to the eerie aura surrounding the Appalachian Tunnels, reinforcing the idea that there's more to these mountains than meets the eye.

CONCLUSION

In concluding our journey through the pages of *Appalachian Folklore Unveiled*, we find ourselves standing at the crossroads of history, culture, and the timeless stories that define the Appalachian region. The tales woven into the fabric of these hills and valleys are not mere stories; they are living, breathing entities that echo the footsteps of those who came before us.

As we peel back the layers of time, we unearth the resilience of a people shaped by isolation, economic trials, and the majesty of the Appalachian Trail, a path that weaves hikers and tourists into the very heart of this enchanting landscape. Through the lens of literature and the arts, we discover the profound impact of authors such as Ron Rash and Charles Frazier, artists whose creations mirror the soul of Appalachia.

Delving deeper into the roots, we explore the profound influence of enslaved West Africans on Appalachian folklore, a heritage intertwined with the very essence of these hills. The myriad creatures and spirits that populate the region's myths tell stories of a rich cultural history, where the supernatural is as much a part of daily life as the sunrise over the mountains.

The significance of omens, signs, and the ethereal beings that populate these tales speaks to the connection between the seen and the unseen, a bridge between the material and the mystical. The Nûñnë'hï, a shared legend embodying the fusion of Native American, European, and African American influences, stands as a testament to the diverse nature of Appalachian folklore.

Appalachian cuisine, with its roots deeply embedded in the soil of the region, tells tales of sustenance, resourcefulness, and a love for the land. From the iconic biscuits to the culinary traditions that traverse the mountains, every dish narrates a story of survival and celebration.

The craftsmen of Appalachia, from woodworking to basket weaving, pottery to quilting, have etched their tales into the very materials they shape. Their creations are not merely objects; they are echoes of tradition, each stroke and stitch a tribute to a cultural heritage that persists through time.

As we unveil the layers of Appalachian folklore, we come to understand that this is more than a collection of stories; it is a living, breathing organism of lore that echoes through the valleys, resonating with the laughter of generations, the whispers of spirits, and the rustle of leaves in the wind. The legends of the Appalachian region are not confined to the pages of this book; they continue to evolve, to shape, and to enchant those who venture into the heart of this enduring landscape. May these tales linger in your thoughts, inviting you to explore further, to unravel the mysteries, and to become part of the ongoing story that is Appalachian folklore.

ABOUT THE AUTHORS

Darkness Prevails is a spooky storyteller extraordinaire hailing from the Ozarks of Arkansas. When he's not busy spinning yarns about things that go bump in the night on Eeriecast: The Horror Podcast Network, or on his wildly successful YouTube channel, *Darkness Prevails*, he can often be found wandering through the misty woods, searching for evidence of Bigfoot (or at least an excuse to use his night-vision goggles).

Despite his fascination with the unknown, Darkness Prevails is also a devoted family man. He is the proud father of two terrors-in-training. His wife, who may or may not be a vampire, supports his creepy pursuits and even helps him research his latest hair-raising tales.

With a love for all things spooky and a knack for making even the bravest of souls quiver in their boots, Darkness Prevails is a force to be reckoned with in the horror genre.

Carman Carrion, a dedicated folklore enthusiast and the host of the *Freaky Folklore* and *Destination Terror* podcasts, is a storyteller with a passion for the mysterious and the supernatural. Hailing from Bella Vista, Arkansas, Carman combines a love for writing with an insatiable curiosity about the darker side of storytelling.

Most days are spent in the cozy confines of the office, accompanied by two dogs, Gidget and Oni, tirelessly researching folklore spanning the globe and crafting chilling narratives. With a love for writing and an insatiable curiosity about the darker side of storytelling, Carman Carrion weaves tales that captivate and intrigue, inviting listeners and readers alike to journey into the realms of the unknown.

In addition to her podcasts, Carman, along with her husband, seizes every opportunity to travel across the US, embarking on journeys that unravel the rich mosaic of history and folklore woven into the fabric of our country. Whether exploring tales from the comfort of her office or venturing into the eerie corners of the nation, Carman Carrion invites listeners and readers alike to join her on an intriguing journey into the unknown.

RESOURCES

BOOKS

Appalachian Magazine. *Appalachian Magazine's Mountain Superstitions, Ghost Stories & Haint Tales: A Collection of Memories & Commentaries from the Mountains of Appalachia.* Independently published, 2018.

Brosi, George. *Appalachian Gateway: An Anthology of Contemporary Stories and Poetry.* Edited by Kate Egerton. Tennessee: University of Tennessee Press, 2013.

Chase, Richard. *The Jack Tales.* Houghton Mifflin Harcourt Books for Young Readers: Massachusetts, 1993.

Edited by Mari-Lynn Evans, Robert Santelli, Holly George-Warren. *The Appalachians: America's First and Last Frontier.* New York, NY: Random House, 2004.

Guess, Justin H. *Old and New Southern Appalachian Urban Legends, Tales, Cryptids, and Monsters: Southern Appalachian Folklore.* Independently published, 2023.

Milnes, Gerald. *Signs, Cures, and Witchery: German Appalachian Folklore.* University of Tennessee Press, 2007.

O'Keefe, Pat Bussard. *Appalachian Granny Witch Magick: Magick and Musings of an Appalachian Mountain Witch.* Alabama: Reaper Publishing, 2023.

Randall, Mark A. *West Virginia Cryptids: A Visual Travel Guide for Traversing the Mountain State.* Independently published by Mark A. Randall, 2021.

Randolph, Vance. *We always lie to strangers: Tall tales from the Ozarks.* Oxford, England: Oxford University Press, 1951.

Rehder, B. John. *Appalachian Folkways.* Johns Hopkins University Press, 2004.

Richards, Jake. *Ossman & Steel's Classic Household Guide to Appalachian Folk Healing: A Collection of Old-Time Remedies, Charms, and Spells.* Massachusetts: Weiser Books, 2022.

Richmond, Nancy. *Appalachian Folklore: Omens, Signs and Superstitions.* CreateSpace Independent Publishing Platform, 2011.

Stockton, Steve. *Strange Things in The Woods: A Collection of Terrifying Tales.* Beyond the Fray Publishing, 2020.

Southgate, Emily, W. B. *People and the Land through Time: Linking Ecology and History.* Connecticut: Yale University Press, 2019.

Williams, John Alexander. *Appalachia: A History.* North Carolina: The University of North Carolina Press, 2002.

Wigginton, Eliot, et al. *Foxfire 2: Ghost Stories, Spring Wild Plant Foods, Spinning and Weaving, Midwifing, Burial Customs, Corn Shuckin's, Wagon Making and More Affairs of Plain Living.* Anchor Books, 1973.

WEBSITES AND DIGITAL ARCHIVES

American Folklore: https://www.americanfolklore.net/

"Appalachian Ghost Stories in Mountain Culture." The Moonlit Road. Traveling the Strange South Through Storytelling. January 12, 2024. https://www.themoonlitroad.com/appalachian-mountain-culture-ghost-stories/.

Appalachian State University Library. Special Collections Research Center. "Folklife and Folklore." January 1, 2024. https://collections.library.appstate.edu/research-aids/subjects/folklife-and-folklore.

Appalachian Studies Association. July 11, 2023. https://www.appalachianstudies.org/.

"Belhurst Castle Joins Haunted History Trail of New York State." Life in the Finger Lakes. September 5, 2018. www.lifeinthefingerlakes.com/belhurst-castle-joins-haunted-history-trail-of-new-york-state/.

Belief Hole. "Appalachian Magic and Haints in the Holler." Belief Hole Podcast. Podcast audio. Accessed June 3, 2024. https://beliefhole.com/appalachian-magic-and-haints-in-the-holler

Blue Ridge Institute, "A New Look at the Past." January 1, 2024. https://blueridgeinstitute.org/.

Bret Love and Mary Gabbett, "The Appalachian Culture & History of the Blue Ridge Mountains." Blue Ridge National Heritage Area, JB Media Group. November 15, 2020. https://blueridgemountainstravelguide.com/appalachian-culture-and-history/.

Chi Luu, "The Legendary Language of the Appalachian 'Holler.'" JSTOR Daily. August 8, 2018. https://daily.jstor.org/the-legendary-language-of-the-appalachian-holler/.

Cieslik, Emma. "Appalachian Folk Magic: Generations of 'Granny Witchcraft' and Spiritual Work." Smithsonian Center for Folklife and Cultural Heritage. August 15,. 2023. folklife.si.edu/magazine/appalachian-folk-magic.

Dave Tabler, "'Everyday' Appalachian Superstitions." Appalachian History. October 12, 2020. https://www.appalachianhistory.net/2020/10/everyday-appalachian-superstitions.html#:~:text=Here%20are%20some%20%E2%80%9Ceveryday%E2%80%9D%20superstitions,to%20void%20the%20bad%20luck.

Digital Library of Appalachia. December 12, 2023. https://dla.contentdm.oclc.org/.

Emma Cieslik, "Appalachian Folk Magic: Generations of 'Granny Witchcraft' and Spiritual Work." Smithsonian Center for Folklife & Cultural Heritage. August 15, 2023. https://folklife.si.edu/magazine/appalachian-folk-magic.

Kelly Kazek, "19 Pieces of Mountain Folklore for Everyday Life." It's a Southern Thing. January 14, 2020. https://www.southernthing.com/appalachian-folklore-2644725912.html.

Lawrence, Beth. "View of Hot Springs, NC Lovers." The Sylvan Herald. October 25, 2023. https://www.thesylvaherald.com/news/article_63be7a46-193a-11eb-bcb1-9b6452791b80.html

Legends of America: https://www.legendsofamerica.com/

Lewis Powell IV, "Thomas Divide Ghost Lights." Southern Spirit Guide. December 16. 2018. www.southernspiritguide.org/thomas-divide-ghost-lights/.

Madison Whipple, "What is Appalachian Culture?" The Collector. October 16, 2023. https://www.thecollector.com/what-is-appalachian-culture/.

Margaret Hester, "The Thomas Divide." The Western Carolinian. November 10, 2006. www.westerncarolinian.com/2006/11/10/the-thomas-divide/.

Museum of Appalachia. "A Living Mountain Village." February 2, 2024. https://www.museumofappalachia.org/.

NCpedia. "View of Hot Springs, NC Lovers." NCpedia. Accessed June 6, 2024. https://www.ncpedia.org/media/view-hot-springs-nc-lovers

Roadtrippers. "Lovers Leap View." Accessed June 3, 2024. https://maps.roadtrippers.com/us/hot-springs-nc/nature/lovers-leap-view.

Southern Spirit Guide: A Guide to the Ghosts and Hauntings of the American South. January 21, 2024. www.southernspiritguide.org/.

Taylor, Traci. "Upstate New York Castle Has Quite the Haunted History." 98.1 The Hawk. October 26, 2023. 981thehawk.com/belhurst-castle-haunted-room/.

The Enlightenment Journey. "Appalachian Folktales: Ghosts, Witches, and Haunted Hollers." The Enlightenment Journey. April 13, 2024. theenlightenmentjourney.com/appalachian-folktales-ghosts-witches-and-haunted-hollers/.

"The Haunted Belhurst Castle, Geneva, NY." Haunted Rooms America. April 15, 2022. www.hauntedrooms.com/new-york/haunted-places/haunted-hotels/belhurst-castle.

Wigington, Patti. "Appalachian Folk Magic and Granny Witchcraft." Learn Religions. December 28, 2019. www.learnreligions.com/appalachian-folk-magic-4779929.

INDEX

First published in 2024 by Wellfleet Press an imprint of The Quarto Group,
142 West 36th Street, 4th Floor, New York, NY 10018, USA
(212) 779-4972 www.Quarto.com

Wellfleet titles are also available at discount for retail, wholesale, promotional, and bulk purchase. For details, contact the Special Sales Manager by email at specialsales@quarto.com or by mail at The Quarto Group, Attn: Special Sales Manager, 100 Cummings Center Suite 265D, Beverly, MA 01915 USA.

10 9 8 7 6 5 4 3 2 1

ISBN: 978-1-57715-440-2

Digital edition published in 2024
eISBN: 978-0-7603-8989-8

Library of Congress Cataloging-in-Publication Data

Names: Darkness Prevails, author. | Carman Carrion, author.
Title: Appalachian folklore unveiled : mysterious happenings of folk
   spirits and mystic shades from the ancient foothills / Darkness Prevails
   with Carman Carrion.
Description: New York : Wellfleet Press, 2024. | Includes bibliographical
   references and index. | Summary: "Told by master storytellers Darkness
   Prevails and Carman Carrion, Appalachian Folklore Unveiled explores the
   mysteries behind Appalachian folklore, ghosts, creepy creatures,
   superstitions, and omens, walking the reader through a little-known land
   of magic and lore that stretches from Canada to the Southern United
   States"-- Provided by publisher.
Identifiers: LCCN 2024010258 (print) | LCCN 2024010259 (ebook) | ISBN
   9781577154402 (hardcover) | ISBN 9780760389898 (ebook)
Subjects: LCSH: Folklore--Appalachian Region. | Legends--Appalachian
   Region. | Ghosts--Appalachian Region. | Tales--Appalachian Region.
Classification: LCC GR108.15 .D37 2024 (print) | LCC GR108.15 (ebook) |
   DDC 398.0974--dc23/eng/20240323
LC record available at https://lccn.loc.gov/2024010258
LC ebook record available at https://lccn.loc.gov/2024010259

Group Publisher: Rage Kindelsperger
Editorial Director: Erin Canning
Creative Director: Laura Drew
Managing Editor: Cara Donaldson
Editors: Sara Bonacum and Keyla Pizarro-Hernández
Art Director: Scott Richardson
Cover and Interior Design: Annie Marino

Printed in China